CIVIL
AVIATION
a design history

CIVIL AVIATION

a design history

DON MIDDLETON

LONDON

IAN ALLAN LTD

Contents

Designed by Ged Casserly

First published 1986

ISBN 0 7110 1515 5

Published by Ian Allan Ltd,
Shepperton, Surrey;
and printed by Ian Allan
Printing Ltd at their works
at Coombelands in Runnymede,
England

Foreword
By **Sir Peter Masefield** *MA, CEng, Hon DSc, Hon DTech, Hon FRAeS*

Design is at the heart of the civil aviation business; it is the basis of the performance of aircraft and their systems, and a major factor in their economic efficiency. Design projects the image of an airline. It is at the centre of an aircraft's and an airline's appeal to customers. It engenders interest and pride among the staff of manufacturers and operators alike. And all that is true of airports and the whole infrastructure of aviation affairs.

Thus, the importance of good design and of good design-management is even more important in aviation than in most other activities.

Don Middleton has performed an important and most welcome service in his review of design as it applies to all these aspects — from its beginnings in the early airship days before World War 1 down to the present times of the wide-bodied jets and the supersonic Concorde and of the major international airports across the world.

Down the years, aircraft design has been dominated by the requirements of technology in increasingly sophisticated aerodynamics and in steadily more advanced structural methods and materials. Against that background, aircraft liveries — as with other abstract applications — have moved in fashions from the early and insensitive application of large registration letters and company names on wings and fuselages to — the sometimes equally insensitive — application of specific motifs and garish colours.

In among the clutter, a few classic examples shine out. In aerodynamics (but not in structures) there was the de Havilland DH91 Albatross. In structures (but not in aerodynamics) there was the Junkers Ju52. In both aerodynamics and structures, there is Concorde.

Among the 'tools of the trade' one must record, down the years, the Northrop Alpha of 1930, the Boeing 247 of 1932 — the first of the modern formula — the DC-3 of 1936 (the first 'economic' airliner), the Boeing 707 of 1954 and the Boeing 747 of 1969 (the first of the 'wide bodies').

As with aircraft, so in airline motifs, there have been some classic examples — prominent among them the twin 'Speedbird' of Imperial Airways, later simplified into BOAC's single 'Speedbird'; regrettably (to my mind) now abandoned by British Airways.

The first of the — almost universally adopted — 'white tops' was applied by Pan American Airways to its Constellation 079 aircraft in 1946. It was a practical, as well as an elegant, example of design ingenuity because, under a hot sun on an airport apron, a white top keeps the cabin interior several degrees cooler than does any other colour.

All the way through, design is a subject on which there can be many views and opinions. There is a general accord, however, that there is a long-term appeal in simplicity, often missed in temporarily fashionable 'business'. There have been some notable aberrations too. For example, after leading the way in its application of good design to its first Elizabethan Class Airspeed Ambassadors and its pioneering Vickers Viscount turbo-props, British European Airways went on to adopt a totally unsympathetic and static square symbol for the abbreviation 'BEA' on its tail, wholly out of keeping with the flowing lines of the aircraft.

Other examples can be found elsewhere.

The fact is, good design does not happen of itself. It has to be inspired and, as in other directions, professionalism counts.

Among those who should be remembered for their contributions; in aerodynamics are Sydney Camm, Geoffrey de Havilland, Arthur Hagg, Hall Hibberd, John K. Northrop, Bailey Oswald, Archibald Russell and Barnes Wallis; on aircraft interiors, Bob Morgan of BEA; and at airports, Terence Conran, Freddy Gibberd and Philip Gordon-Marshall — to name only a few.

Design in civil aviation embraces a very wide field of expertise — some of it superlative, some of it less good. May I commend this book by Don Middleton as a comprehensive review of the most significant contributions, not only to modern technology, but to aesthetic appearances as well. It brings out clearly how some of the earnest toilers in this field have succeeded — how some have not.

Introduction

The appearance of consumer goods is an integral part of the marketing operation, they may look attractive or unattractive, according to the skill of the design practitioner. If the product is avowedly aesthetic in its appeal, with only a secondary functional requirement, his talents may be directed primarily towards appearance, with ease and economy of production as secondary design parameters. However, the more complex the product and its function, the greater will be the involvement of the engineer, until, at the end of the design spectrum represented by, for example, the space satellite, no aesthetic criteria are involved.

The modern aeroplane comes much nearer to that end of the spectrum but, in its design process, there is scope for beauty. It is interesting to observe the way in which function determines a form which, in the hands of an artist, can be a creation of great beauty; Concorde is a classic example. It is also significant that some aircraft designers, whose training and background embraced the purely technical disciplines, acquired the ability to see a complex machine in aesthetic terms which, happily, were synonymous with a high level of functional efficiency.

Bill Stout, who designed in 1925, the classic Ford Trimotor — known as the 'Tin Goose' — defined an airliner as 'a machine capable of supporting itself financially and aerodynamically at the same time'. The definition has never been improved upon and within it is a complex equation with its elements interdependent upon each other — safety, reliability, comfort, speed, capital cost and operating cost are parts of the whole. So compromise is the name of the game.

The introduction of new constructional techniques can greatly affect the total concept of the aircraft, for example, the discovery of a simple technique of fabricating and manipulating stainless steel sheet would ease the immense difficulties inherent in building a Mach 3 or 4 airliner; such a development would then introduce further problems with other materials subjected to the high kinetic heating levels which would be experienced at such speeds. The engine manufacturers would also be called upon to make considerable technological advances in propulsion methods, particularly in the field of fuel economy.

In this book, the author has endeavoured to trace the process of design evolution in its widest sense, from the early years of air transport. It is a vast subject, so within the confines of the publisher's brief, it has been necessary to leave out some interesting projects and material received from various sources, to whom an apology is due.

As a leading authority on air transport, Sir Peter Masefield's interest in commenting on the manuscript, and in writing the Foreword, is greatly appreciated.

Many companies, airlines and airport authorities have been generous in providing data and photographs. Particular thanks are due to Ron Wilson of British Airways, Michael Brown, Hugh Field and Darryl Cott of British Aerospace, Hatfield, Harry Holmes of BAe Woodford and Norman Barfield of BAe Weybridge, Michael Evans and Jack Titley of Rolls-Royce, Barbara Kracht of Airbus Industrie, Garry May of British Airports Authority, Gunnell Thörne of SAS, Horst Burgmuller of Lufthansa, John Horsman of Gates-Learjet, Harry Fraser-Mitchell of the Handley Page Association, John Stroud and Richard Riding, editor of *Aeroplane Monthly*, as always, a ready fount of wisdom and source of photographs.

Various officials of the national aeronautical research establishments have offered valuable advice and data.

Finally, the author records his appreciation of the assistance of his wife and Hilda Benham, in correcting the manuscript.

Don Middleton

1

Design Considerations

How far does good design, which must be implicit in the title of this book, apply in civil aviation? Indeed, what is meant by the term and by what criteria may it be judged?

Good design, like peace, can be said to be indivisible, certainly there is no part of the airline business where it is irrelevant. Fortunately aviation is a new industry so it does not carry the burden of inheritance from the Industrial Revolution which, for many years, inhibited much of British graphic and industrial design.

The design brief will be predominantly that of the transport vehicle itself, the aeroplane: its servicing facilities, passenger handling amenities and the complex systems of electronic control essential to safe and efficient air travel. In supporting roles will be found the architect, the interior designer and the graphic designer handling the overall environment of the passenger and the airline staff within the philosophy of public relations and advertising which are major elements in the commercial success of an airline.

What constitutes beauty in an industrial product? In ancient Greece Pythagoras and Plato developed a numerical theory of proportion which they saw in natural forms such as crystals, shells, plants and flowers. Their views were embodied in the theory of the Golden Section, a canon of composition and form used in Greek architecture, sculpture and pottery: Roman art was a manifestation of it, the Renaissance was fascinated by it and Ruskin developed from it his theory that all beautiful lines are drawn through mathematical laws organically developed.

Fitness for Purpose was a definition affirmed as long ago as 1915 by the Design and Industries Association, one of the pioneers of the modern movement. In 1922 the DIA addressed itself to the problems of aircraft and published in its Yearbook an interior photograph of a contemporary airliner accompanied by the caption, 'The interior of the aeroplane fusilage (sic) is moulded by the necessity for strong and light construction. The continuous oval frames meet this necessity and are rightly spaced to suit the arrangements of seats, giving to every one a window view and allowing free movement. The symmetry of the resulting design has elements of beauty'.

Whilst this particular application of the slogan 'Fitness for Purpose' is valid, the slogan itself is tenuous in its definition of beauty as a part of the whole. A later definition, 'the promise of function' is equally unsatisfactory for the same reason whilst the popular bromide 'What looks right is right' is palpably untrue in the context of complex technical products such as aircraft. Certainly there have been some extremely efficient aeroplanes which looked superb but there have also been some handsome ones which left much to be desired on technical and operational grounds.

The shape of birds evolved according to their fitness for purpose, the long distance flyers are well streamlined with high aspect ratio wings for optimum aerodynamic efficiency, beauty is inherent in their appearance. Most fish, similarly, have evolved a shape to give maximum performance in their denser medium, again a beautiful shape has usually resulted. Fitness for purpose in its relevance to a civil airliner is a much more intricate concept. The fundamental requirement is that it shall carry its passengers, crew and freight swiftly, comfortably and safely with a very high level of reliability whilst making adequate profit for its manufacturers, owners and operators.

The aeroplane is only as good as its ancillary services, whether internal or external. Its construction must be such that maintenance is as simple as its immensely complicated nature will permit. Efficient staging facilities must be provided in the hangar to facilitate a quick turnround. Special tools must be provided to speed up servicing of airframe and engines which must be capable of rapid replacement if necessary. The airliner is

only creating profit when it is in the air with its complement of passengers. Every hour spent on the ground is an additional expense to the operator.

Some airliners are capable of conversion to freight carriers. The assembly of internal furnishings is ingenious and permits a full conversion in a very short time, similarly the seating plan may be altered at will to accommodate more or fewer first class passengers or a proportion of freight.

The executive transport aircraft has developed rapidly in line with international business activities, in every respect it is a miniature airliner with the same standard of technology but very much higher standards of comfort.

Having landed his aircraft the airline pilot must be aware of the quickest route from the runway to the terminal building under all weather conditions; if movable piers are to be used to disembark passengers he must be directed to a precise spot for alignment of the pier end. This must be deployed quickly with no risk of damage to the aeroplane. Passengers, with their hand luggage, must be able to disembark at once.

Cleaning the interior of the cabin and servicing of galleys and toilets must be carried out swiftly as must the re-fuelling operation and rectification of any minor defects reported by the incoming pilot. All these operations, vital to an efficient airline, must receive consideration whilst the aeroplane is on the drawing board as must one of the most vital requirements,

survival of the occupants in the event of an accident.

Survival introduces other outside technical disciplines into the design team. Although the accident rate on scheduled services is remarkably low the highest risk is present during the take-off and landing phase. Many such accidents are survivable provided that fire fighting and rescue services can reach the scene in time. So, in addition to adequate passenger escape hatches and well trained cabin crews, fire fighting equipment capable of rapid transit over rough terrain and the ability to deluge the aircraft with foam is a vital part of the services at any airport.

One of the major frustrations of air travel in the 1980s is the congestion in airport passenger concourses. There can be no question that passenger handling has not kept pace with the growth of air travel and the vast increase in aircraft capacity. The irritating necessity of arriving at the airport up to two hours before flight departure is quite intolerable and partly negates the advantages of air travel — in two hours the average jet airliner can fly over a thousand miles.

These are some of the problems facing designers in civil aviation. Nothing has been said of the immensely complex radio communication and flight control systems, in short, avionics. Inertial guidance has revolutionised air travel over long haul routes by techniques of electronic wizardry inconceivable 30 years ago. This requires yet another design discipline in electronic engineering, completely untrammelled by

1
First flown in April 1919, the Vickers Vimy Commercial was a development of the Vimy bomber with two 360hp Rolls-Royce Eagle engines. With a range of 450 miles it could carry 10 passengers at a maximum speed of 103mph. 43 were built. *Vickers*

2
The cabin of the Vimy
Commercial. *Vickers*

aesthetic considerations other than in the presentation of the appropriate data upon the flightdeck.

Data presentation is a very important area of aircraft design. The degree of instrumentation on the flightdeck of a modern airliner is awesome but being rapidly reduced by automation and electronic control leaving the pilots with only the instrumentation necessary to monitor the performance of the avionic systems which have been programmed with the required details of the flight to be made. Automatic warning signals indicate malfunctions for which there are clearly defined remedial procedures.

Prior to take-off the pilots spend a considerable amount of time following a check list which covers every vital function of the aeroplane. All of these aspects of design are dealt with at the drawing board stage and later confirmed during the flight test programme.

Once the broad detail of the new airliner is settled by the aerodynamic, structural and economic criteria a 'mock-up' is built. This is a full scale model, usually of wood, which enables the designers to verify the main operational features such as flightdeck layout, seating, toilets and galleys. This must not be confused with the wind tunnel model; this is an exceptionally

accurate replica, probably 15ft in span, from which the aerodynamic characteristics of the aircraft can be investigated. Together with computer and simulator studies a very clear picture of the performance of the new design will emerge and detailed drawings may be completed, aided by the ubiquitous computer, which can produce exceptionally complex drawings of great accuracy in a fraction of the time taken by normal draughting methods. As well as the extreme accuracy of the technique a component may easily be reproduced in perspective and one drawing may be superimposed upon another — for example an electrical layout may be compared with a hydraulic pipe layout to ensure that parts of one do not foul the other.

From these drawings the mock-up is built, often with one wing and the engine installation on one side. In some cases — Concorde was one of them, the mock-up is an elaborate structure, almost indistinguishable internally and externally from the finished aeroplane, and capable of being used to show airline executives exactly what they will receive in exchange for their many millions of pounds — a very valuable public relations exercise. British Aircraft Corporation at Filton achieved a very dramatic effect with their Concorde mock-up by installing it in a hangar with no internal lighting. As one entered the hangar, approaching the port side of the nose of Concorde, the lights were slowly turned up to reveal this beautiful white aeroplane.

The flightdeck mock-up is used to permit airline pilots to express their opinion of control and instrumentation layout so that modifications at prototype stage are reduced to the minimum. In parallel with all these important activities the engineers are producing test rigs for all the services to be installed in the new airliner to ensure that by the time the test pilot is ready to fly it for the first time it is as reliable as human ingenuity can make it. A major programme of structural testing will also have been carried out on components and on one of the prototypes which will spend its life in a huge test rig where flight stresses can be simulated under all conditions of loading and manoeuvre. These tests will continue long after the airliner has gone into service, to determine the fatigue life of the airframe, in other words, the number of hours it may be flown before the risk of fatigue failure in any part of the structure becomes unacceptable. A new hazard arises in the case of aircraft designed for supersonic speed, the structure will be heated to a high temperature by its passage through the air so it is essential that the effect of thermal stress is investigated very thoroughly. Structural testing of Concorde was carried out in a rig where rapid cycles of heating and cooling could be simulated.

The engines and avionics of the aircraft will also be undergoing tests both on the bench and in flying test beds to ensure that the utmost reliability is achieved before the important first flight and the intensive flight test programme which will follow.

From the foregoing the sheer volume of technical effort involved in the design of civil aircraft will be apparent. Other aspects of the air transport industry also require a considerable design effort.

Airport terminal buildings, planned, it is hoped, to achieve an efficient flow of passengers to and from their aeroplane with adequate facilities for baggage retrieval, toilets, shops, restaurants and car parking should have a very clear public address system with adequate audio-visual aids to indicate flight departure and arrival times. All these are part of the design effort

in which aesthetics can and do play a very important role. The crucially important control tower with its responsibility for the safe arrival and departure of millions of travellers is a complex exercise in air traffic control and in avionics technology at its highest level, but one in which the air traffic controller, with his heavy responsibility, is the vital link in the control loop.

A national airline is, by its nature, a major prestige element in the economy of its parent country and most managements are well aware of the importance of their role in projecting a favourable image. National characteristics may be embodied in the way that Air India stewardesses wear beautiful saris whilst Japanese Airlines reflect the national tradition in the style of clothing worn by their stewardesses. Aircraft interiors are designed to be distinctive but restful, the 'tube look' in the smaller jet airliners is often disguised by banks of seats in different colours or by strong horizontal patterns in the seat coverings as in the British Aerospace BAe146.

Most airlines have a logotype, a convention which began in 1919 when Deutsche Luft Reederei, a predecessor of Lufthansa, applied to the rudder of its AEG JIIs the famous flying crane symbol which, in only slightly modified form, may be seen in a yellow circle upon Lufthansa aircraft today. The symbol is carried through the whole of the publicity material, on posters, brochures, letter headings, tickets, vehicles and staff uniform badges. Associated with the logo will be a particular style of lettering which will be applied to every thing from the aeroplane to the baggage labels. It is customary for airlines to issue a 'design bible' which clearly defines all these elements in the design philosophy of the company and ensures consistency in its application. The overall success of the 'image creators' will be apparent to anyone who pauses, as a spectator, for an hour or so at an international airport.

Later chapters will trace the evolution of the design process of the aeroplane and the later involvement of the ancillary services in that process. The growth of the business executive aircraft has been rapid since World War 2, so it, too, will be studied with the helicopter and other special purpose aeroplanes of particular interest from the design viewpoint.

2

The Adventurous Years

This chapter will study the development of commercial aviation in the 1930s, a period which set the stage for the spectacular growth of air travel which has, quite literally, changed the world. It is interesting to realise that, even at this early stage, such facilities as in-flight catering and heated cabins were offered to the intrepid passengers.

The first postwar British airline was Air Transport and Travel, formed by George Holt Thomas whose Aircraft Manufacturing Company (Airco) had produced, before the war, Farman aircraft under licence. Capt Geoffrey de Havilland was his chief designer. His DH2, DH4 and DH9 were built by Airco.

Captain Jerry Shaw of AT&T, as the company was known, flew the first service — or charter, to be quite precise — on 15 July 1919, the day on which civil flying received Government authority to operate under the provisions of the International Convention for Aerial Navigation. The first passenger was Col W. N. Pilkington, of the St Helens glass firm, who had to go to Paris on business at short notice. Shaw's DH9 left Hendon at 07.30, broke the rules by failing to clear Customs at Hounslow Heath, flew via Folkestone and Dover to Beauvais, rarely climbing above 2,000ft and landed at Le Bourget 2¾ hours later.

On 25 August 1919, a DH4A made the first scheduled international flight from London to Paris and Maj Cyril Palleson flew four passengers to Paris in a DH16 — a modified DH9 — cutting Shaw's flight time by 15min. Other airlines which commenced operations in 1919 were Handley Page Transport (HPT), set up by Frederick Handley Page to create a larger market for his own aeroplanes, and the Instone Airlines, an off-shoot of the shipping and colliery empire of Sir Samuel Instone. Both operated across the English Channel, HPT using a converted O/400 bomber, making

3, 4
LZ127 *Graf Zeppelin* which on 18 May 1930 crossed the South Atlantic non-stop from Seville, Spain, to Recife, Brazil. In 1932 it entered into regular service between Friedrichshafen and Recife. *Lufthansa*

its first non-scheduled flight on 25 August and beginning a thrice-weekly service on 2 September. Three weeks later, a service to Brussels began, the British terminal being the Handley Page aerodrome at Cricklewood.

In October the line achieved another distinction as the first airline to introduce in-flight catering — for 3/6, (17½p) a lunch box was provided, containing six sandwiches, fruit and chocolate, a nourishing repast for those whose digestion was equal to the turbulent and bumpy ride.

Instone Airlines started by accident. Delays to ship's papers at French ports and elsewhere caused expensive delays to the vessels so Instone decided to seek Government permission to fly the documentation to the ships in the company's own aeroplane. Permission was given and, surprisingly, the Air Ministry offered Instone a DH4 and pilot. He was Franklyn L. Barnard who was later appointed chief pilot of Instone and, ultimately, chief pilot of Imperial Airways. Capt Barnard piloted a DH4A on the London to Paris route in February 1920 and two months later took delivery of the Vickers Vimy Commercial, a modified Vimy bomber with a capacious new fuselage capable of accommodating 10 passengers in a fair degree of comfort. Removal of the seats gave a freight carrying capacity of 2,500lb.

The provision of a covered cockpit for the pilots aroused considerable controversy, indeed, acrimony, in these early days. The Vimy Commercial was designed with a covered cockpit but violent objections by the test pilot resulted in reversion to an open cockpit before first flight. Handley Page's O/400 was built, in one version, with an enclosure. Capt Wally Hope was the first pilot to fly it, the conditions were very bumpy en route to Paris. He hated being enclosed and demanded that the canopy should be removed as he liked to 'feel the wind on his face'. Being an impatient man, he took matters into his own hands and demolished it with an axe!

Not until 1931, when the Handley Page HP42 went into production, was an enclosed cockpit seen on a British airliner.

In Germany, supposedly on 11 November 1918, the day the Great War ended, Hugo Junkers instructed his design staff under Otto Reuter to cease work on military aircraft and design a civil transport. Already in production was the J10 two-seat fighter of advanced design with an all-metal structure and a cantilever low wing.

In March 1919 Junkers used a modified J10, without armament and fitted with a canopy over the rear cockpit to protect the single passenger, to inaugurate their own airline service between Dessau and Weimar. It is almost certain that the distinction of operating the first all-metal commercial aeroplane on a scheduled route must go to Junkers.

Professor Junkers and Herr Reuter, in the meantime, were designing and building the famous J13, soon to be known as the F13, and first flown on 25 June 1919. This historic design was the first all-metal, cantilever monoplane to go into service anywhere in the world. It was unique as its peers were all biplanes with a considerable number of drag producing struts and bracing wires.

Another interesting contemporary German design was the Rohrbach E4/20. A four-engined high wing monoplane, it was built almost entirely of duralumin. A box spar was the basis of the 'almost' cantilever wing — almost, because the wing loading of 16.4lb/sq ft was high for the period and outside normal experience, so it was decided to fit cables from the underside of the fuselage to the spar, well outboard of the engines.

The specification reads like one from three decades later. Twelve passengers sat

4

5
A converted de Havilland DH4A day bomber similar to the one which opened the world's first scheduled international air service from Hounslow Heath to Le Bourget on 25 August 1919. The pilot on this historic flight was E. H. Lawford; the fare — 20 guineas.

The DH4 carried two passengers, sitting face to face, at a maximum speed of 121mph. *British Airways*

6
Jerry Shaw, one of the pilots on the Air Transport and Travel London to Paris service. *Flight via British Airways*

in paired seats, facing each other, across tables. They enjoyed the view through large windows and had access to a toilet. Baggage and mail holds were provided and the machine carried radio. It originally had an open cockpit but was later fitted with an enclosure.

In September 1920 the test flight programme commenced, the 101ft span machine achieving the very creditable speed of 140mph on one flight with an endurance of over 5hr. At the end of 1922 the Allied Control Commission in Germany decided that the aeroplane infringed the terms of the Versailles Treaty and they ordered its destruction.

Another aircraft of considerable importance in the history of civil aviation was the French Farman Goliath. Powered by two 380hp Bristol Jupiter radial engines made under licence by Gnome Rhône, or by any other similar engines, this 86ft 11in span biplane appeared in 1919, and established world records for altitude, climbing to 16,732ft with 25 passengers, and for distance, with a flight of 1,274 miles from Paris to Casablanca in 18hr with eight occupants.

Normally the Goliath carried up to 12 passengers and a crew of two who were seated in an open cockpit between the two cabins, sparsely furnished with four wicker seats in the forward one — and a splendid view ahead, whilst eight wicker seats were located in the after cabin. The basic structure was a mixed metal and wooden airframe. Early versions of the type had balanced ailerons with the balance areas extending well beyond the wing tips. Later, inset ailerons were fitted. The trailing edges of the wings, elevators and rudder had that curious feature of French aeroplanes of the period, the scalloped profile achieved by allowing the tightening effect of the dope on the wing fabric to pull in the light tubular trailing edge, between the ribs.

The unusual design of spatted undercarriage softened the general ugliness characteristic of so many French aeroplanes. It also revealed the designer's appreciation of the drag caused by undercarriage struts and bracing wires, and set a pattern which was followed by many companies prior to the development of the retractable undercarriage.

In terms of total ugliness, a successor to the Goliath, the Farman Jabiru which first flew in 1923, must be among the leaders. Its fuselage, similar to the Goliath, had a low aspect ratio wooden wing on top, braced to small stub wings at the bottom of the fuselage which carried four 180hp Hispano-Suiza water-cooled engines in two tandem pairs. Cooling problems with the rear pair led to the development of three-engined and twin-engined versions.

The Goliath was introduced at a time when a number of airlines began operations in France. It was used by Compagnie des Grands Express Aeriennes for an early service from Le Bourget to Croydon. Compagnie de Messageries Aeriennes followed CGEA on the route,

operating, with them, a total of 27 Goliaths, the last of which was withdrawn from commercial service in 1933. In 1923 the two companies merged to form Air Union.

Maurice Farman himself started Ligne Farman, another case of a manufacturer taking such a step to sell and publicise the merits of his own aeroplanes. Other users of the Goliath were Syndicat National d'Etudes du Transport Aérien and SNETA, the Belgian line formed in 1920. In 1923 the Belgian Government took over their assets to form SABENA and exploit the routes to the Belgian Congo which had already been opened with six 1917 vintage Levy-Lepen R single-engined flying boats. In the two years which ended in June 1922 and saw the termination of the service to Stanleyville, the boats flew over 77,500 miles carrying 95 passengers and over 4,000lb of mail — a significant indication of the level of achievement in the primitive aviation operations of the period.

7
The Westland Limousine. Westland's first commercial aircraft and one of the earliest attempts to introduce comfort into flying. First flown in 1919, and powered with various engines ranging from a 275hp Rolls-Royce Falcon III to a 450hp Napier Lion, the cruising speed was 85-90mph, with three passengers and the pilot. The Limousine was also offered as a 'Businessman's machine' — a Westland director achieved publicity by dictating letters to his secretary in flight and the lady them typed them whilst the flight continued!

The Limousine won first prize for small aircraft in the Air Ministry Commercial Aeroplane Competition in 1920 but only eight were built. The purpose of the lady's parasol is a little obscure, she may have read about parachutes! The trade mark on the side is an interesting example of graphic design in the 1920s.
Aeroplane Monthly

8

With Hugo Junkers in Germany, the Dutch Fokker company dominated European commercial aviation until the outbreak of World War 2. Their constructional approaches were, however, quite different. Junkers was innovative, using all metal construction whilst Fokker relied upon a mixed structure of ply-covered wooden cantilever wings and welded steel tubular fuselages with wooden stringers to fair-in the fabric covering. It is paradoxical that the end of WW1 terminated Junkers work upon advanced designs of aircraft whilst the much less enterprising Fokker company was quickly revived and continued to build transport aircraft.

After a few FII single-engined, four-passenger aircraft had been built, the FIII appeared in 1920. Following the high cantilever wooden wing formula, over 50 were built and put into service in 1921 with KLM, the recently opened Royal Dutch Airlines and with a number of fledgeling European airlines.

Later, the FVII appeared. Powered by a single 360hp Rolls-Royce Eagle engine this ugly aeroplane was first flown from Schiphol aerodrome on 23 April 1924. It had a very satisfactory performance. To reduce control loads, the ailerons were designed with a part of their area forward of the hinge line, projecting beyond the tip. The elevator design followed the same principle, although on the rudder, the horn balance, as the device was known, was faired into the profile of the fin.

Fokker decided upon a redesign of the basic aircraft and his designer, Reinhold Platz, produced a much more attractive aircraft to be known as FVIIA. This machine, powered by a 400hp Liberty V12 engine made by the Packard company, had accommodation in the cabin for eight passengers whilst the two pilots were in an open cockpit.

Fokker was one of the first aircraft manufacturers to offer a range of different engines for his aeroplanes. He soon realised that the potential of the FVII would be increased substantially if it could be offered with three engines. This version was first flown in September 1925 as the FVII/3M.

(continued)

By 1928 the Czechoslovak line CSA was operating eight Goliaths built under licence in that country by Avia and Letov.

Frederick Handley Page and Geoffrey de Havilland were determined to make their mark in the civil aircraft market. This particularly suited the talents of the gentle and retiring de Havilland who detested war and took no satisfaction from designing military aircraft. HP had no such inhibitions; a pugnacious extrovert, he would build anything likely to show a profit. Various civil developments of the bombers — like the W8 and W10 — emerged from Cricklewood. They gave good service but were underpowered. The problems of poor power/weight ratio caused the passenger loads of these early airliners to be reduced to levels which were

economically fatal for the unsubsidised British carriers competing with the subsidised European lines.

In February 1921 the British operators ceased to fly until the Government relented and provided a subsidy which enabled Handley Page to restart the Paris service in March of that year. The subsidy scheme led, in 1924, to the formation of the national carrier, Imperial Airways Ltd, by the amalgamation of Handley Page Transport, Daimler Airway, Instone and the small British Marine Air Navigation Company with a capital of one million pounds and a subsidy of a similar amount spread over 10 years.

Various disasters emphasised the importance of air traffic control. The necessity of aerodrome lighting and route

marking beacons for night operations was also becoming an urgent matter. Britain was in the forefront of night flying facilities; Hounslow Heath had a light beacon which flashed three times in 10sec and was switched on by request, or if an aircraft was heard in the vicinity. In 1919 a revolving beacon was built and in the next year a flashing beacon was installed at Le Bourget.

Hounslow became inadequate for commercial operations so in March 1920 the old RAF aerodrome at Wallington, south of the capital, was taken over together with another grass aerodrome, Waddon, to the east of it, the two being divided by Plough Lane.

To the west of the lane were the maintenance hangars and administrative huts. Facing the landing area was the Customs Office on top of which the wooden control tower was erected on stilts. A number of temporary canvas hangars were built near the passenger area. One of these collapsed under the weight of snow on it, with dire consequences for the aircraft inside. Airliners had to taxi from the hangars to the passenger terminal over Plough Lane, even negotiating part of a farm in the process!

Aircraft were signalled to take-off by a man with a red flag. To assist landing in fog or at night a neon beacon was installed, neon tubes were sunk into the surface to guide machines landing in poor visibility and a tracked vehicle carrying a floodlight was commissioned.

In 1928 the historic buildings known to

Later to be fitted with a larger wing, fin and rudder it was an immediate success. The two extra engines were fitted to a tubular structure under the wing which also anchored the shortened undercarriage shock-absorbing oleo leg. At least 11 different types of radial engine were fitted. The most famous FVII/3M was Sir Charles Kingsford Smith's *Southern Cross*, in which he made many record-breaking flights. *KLM*

9
The Junkers F13 was the workhorse of the Lufthansa fleet from 1926 to 1932. More than 40 were operated as landplanes — with either wheels or skis — or as seaplanes. The heated cabin accommodated four passengers who were provided with safety belts. Various engines, ranging in power from the 250hp BMW to the 380hp Junkers L5, were offered. The maximum speed was 110mph and the range 400 miles. The Junkers F13 was a classic airliner of immense importance in the development of air transport; approximately 350 were built. *Lufthansa*

10
The Rohrbach Roland I was in Lufthansa service from 1926 to 1935. It embodied many of the design features of the luckless E4/20. The wing bracing may be seen in the photograph, also the metal propellers, made from a slab of twisted duralumin which enabled thin blade sections to be used for greater efficiency, a practice later followed in Britain with the Fairey-Reed metal propeller.

The Roland II appeared in 1929 with three 320hp BMW engines. It carried 10 passengers and a crew of two at a cruising speed of 110mph. Range was 800 miles. *Lufthansa*

11
The Farman Goliath was powered by a variety of engines ranging from the 230hp Salmson radial to the 380hp Gnome-Rhône Jupiter engine.

The span was 86ft 10in and up to 12 passengers were carried in two cabins, the forward one being right in the nose. The crew of two sat in an open cockpit. Maximum speed was 94mph with a range of 250 miles. Over 50 Goliaths were built and some of them served the airlines until 1933. *Air France via John Stroud*

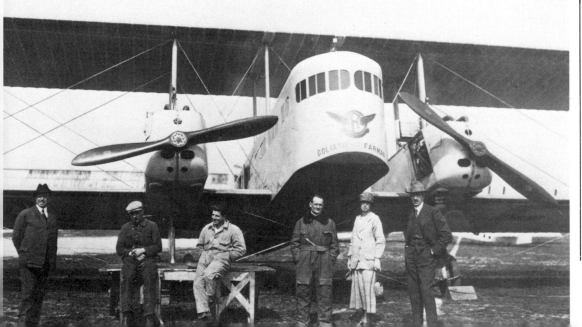

12
The interior of a Farman Goliath looking from the aft cabin to the nose accommodation. Note the wire bracing along the cabin sides and the anchorage of the centre section bracing wires at the ends of the heavy strut over the seats. Of interest is the Art Nouveau decoration on the cabin sides and bulkhead.
Air France via John Stroud

13
Built as a three and a four engined machine, the Farman 3X Jabiru must surely be the ugliest aeroplane of all time. The engines were Bristol Jupiters, made by Gnome Rhône under licence. It carried a crew of one or two with up to nine passengers. *John Stroud*

14
The interior of the F121 Jabiru, which had four engines.
Collection Air France

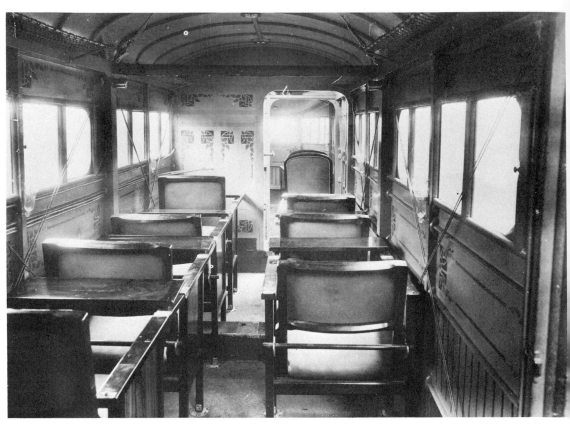

many thousands of air travellers in the 1930s began to appear. Alongside what is now Purley Way, to the east, was built a two storey administration building for the airlines, Customs and Immigration authorities and freight stores. The distinctive control tower was mounted on top. Aerodrome lighting was improved and Plough Lane disappeared to give a landing area 1,450yd from east to west and 1,300yd from north to south with a maximum take-off run of 1,600yd from north east to south west, a run which was hazarded by the presence of rising ground on the south westerly heading, as several pilots, in under-powered aeroplanes found, to their dismay.

In 1926 Air Union began a regular night service from Croydon to Paris before the new facilities were opened in 1928. The airport was known as the Air Port of London-Croydon and formed the prototype of similar airports throughout the world.

All air traffic control was handled from the tower. For the period the system was considered to be highly satisfactory. In the control tower a large map showed the position of all aircraft on the cross-Channel routes by small flags with the registration letters of the machines upon them. Next door was a wireless telegraph operator who was in contact with the

pilots. In poor visibility the pilot might call for a 'fix'. Radio direction finding stations operated at Croydon, Lympne in Kent and at the old airship base at Pulham in Norfolk. The operators could pick up signals from the aircraft and determine its compass bearing from the stations. Weighted strings on a map in the Croydon control tower reproduced the bearings given, and the point at which the strings crossed formed a small triangle within which the aircraft was located to an accuracy of about 1½ miles.

By the end of the decade Croydon had a powerful neon flashing beacon, sunken red neon lights to show the landing area, flashing red lights to indicate the aerodrome boundary, red lights to mark the buildings and other obstructions and a floodlit marshalling area in front of the control tower and hangars. All meteorological services were concentrated in the terminal building.

Passenger facilities were very civilised with airline booking offices in the spacious main hall; a bookstall, Post Office and coffee room were available — the latter was particularly popular as passengers met such characters as Capt O. P. Jones, with his rakish pointed beard, and A. S. Wilcockson, who flew some of the first Imperial Airways flying boat services

13

across the Atlantic; they must have enlivened many passengers' refreshment.

Sir Peter Masefield, in the foreword to Sutton Libraries[7] fascinating history of Croydon airport, calls it 'the first custom-built airport in the world, which fortunately, remains as a monument to 'the great days that were'. It is planned to develop the control and administrative building as a museum. In the present Airport Hotel, which was built as part of the original scheme, can be seen many of the caricatures of the early pilots operating from Croydon.

In its 33 years of active commercial aviation life, Croydon handled 1,900,000 passengers in 650,000 aircraft movements. Sir Peter reports that between 1920 and the outbreak of war in 1939, 1,365,000 passengers were carried in 160,000 aircraft movements, an average of eight per flight. The bulk of the passengers were carried before the war but the majority of the movements took place afterwards, between 1946 and 1959, when its activities were restricted to training, charter and general aviation.

On its inception, Imperial Airways had a mixed bag of aircraft, mainly DH34s, three W8s, a Vickers Vimy Commercial, a Vulcan, a DH4A and two Sea Eagle amphibious flying boats inherited from British Marine

14

15, 16
The Handley Page W10 was the
last of a group of large airliners
developed directly from the
O/400 wartime bomber, which
was hurriedly converted for
civil use when HP started his
own airline, HP Air Transport,
in 1919. The O/400 had already
been used for freight and mail
transport by No 86
(Communications) Wing, RAF
and Handley Page bought back
16 new aircraft from the Air
Ministry as soon as the war
ended; 12 of them were still in
his works being completed. The
four already built were
converted to drop parcels of
newspapers from the bomb bay
by parachute. Seven passengers
could endure an uncomfortable
flight on primitive seats in the
fuselage whilst two more could
make an even more spartan
journey in the front gunner's
cockpit.

The first true civil aircraft,
the O/7, of which 11 were built,
carried 12 passengers, 10 in
inwards-facing wicker chairs
along the sides of the cabin, and
another hardy pair in the front
cockpit ahead of the two pilots
who were also exposed to the
weather. Later, Handley Page
decided to build a mail/freight
version, the O/11, with
provision for five passengers.

In 1920 joyriding began to be
a popular pastime so more
O/400s were converted to carry
10 passengers. One of the most
memorable of this version was
built for an Eastern potentate
who instructed that the interior
be lined with pink silk with the
exterior doped in a high gloss
pink finish, the nacelles being
blue. Predictably, the
Cricklewood workers dubbed it
'the pink elephant'!

In December 1919 the W8 flew
for the first time. This was
Handley Page's first true
airliner with a cabin
unobstructed by internal
bracing tubes. It used many
components of the O/400 and
the larger V/1500 bomber, the
wings being based upon those
of the two machines. Only one
W8 was built and developed
into the W8b. This had two
Rolls-Royce Eagle engines of
350hp each. The well-appointed
cabin seated 14 passengers in
wicker chairs; the floor was
carpeted, whilst electric
candelabra, a clock and a
lavatory added a touch of
luxury to the scene. Large
windows afforded a splendid
view for the passengers who

(continued)

Air Navigation Co (BMANC). It was
intended to develop routes to the Middle
and Far East, so surveys began. That great
airman Alan Cobham was very active in
these survey flights. In the meantime
Armstrong Whitworth built the famous
Argosy three-engined airliner and de
Havilland produced the DH66, similarly
with three engines, and later named
Hercules as a result of a competition to find
a name which was organised by the
Meccano Magazine and won by a boy from
Eton College.

On 29 July 1926 the first Argosy left
Croydon for Paris with 18 passengers. Its
flight time was 1hr 51min — whereas the
O/400s took nearly 3hr. When Imperial
Airways was formed the various colour
schemes of the constituent operators were
changed to a standard royal blue fuselage
with aluminium doped wings and tail. The
Argosies were later painted in aluminium
dope with royal blue trim. Their attractive
colours belied the discomfort of flying in
them. The noise from the engines was
appalling, with vibration from the nose
engine transmitted through the fuselage;
the wing bracing wires — accompanied by
draughts — came through holes in the
fabric covering of the steel tube fuselage.

In the cabin roof were ripping panels for
escape in the event of a crash. All too often
these became dripping panels in wet
weather. The passengers sat on wicker
chairs in a spacious cabin 29ft long, 6ft 3in
high and 4ft 6in wide. Each seat was
alongside an opening window. The pilots,
as in the DH Hercules, remained, at their
own insistence, in open cockpits.

At the end of 1926 the first Hercules was
delivered, within 12 months of the
commencement of design — a remarkable
feat on the part of de Havilland. Within
days it had left Croydon, flying to
Heliopolis for service on the Eastern routes
whilst a second one left two days later for
Cairo, a third one following it on Boxing
Day to inaugurate the Royal Mail service.
Crew familiarisation and route proving
were very simple operations in those days.

In his book *Wings across the World*,
Harald Penrose, himself a distinguished
test pilot, tells the story of Franklyn
Barnard landing an Argosy at Croydon, in a
southwesterly gale, arriving like an
autogyro, with no run, in the lee of the
Customs building. The wind was so fierce
that 20 men were required to hold the
machine down. Taxying was almost
impossible so Barnard took off again and

could smoke if they wished. The fuel tanks were mounted above the upper wing in line with the engines. The first W8 entered airline service in 1922. Seven were built, three for HP Transport, the others for Sabena, the Belgian airline. By the aesthetic criteria of the time, the W8 was an attractive aeroplane in its glossy white dope finish. One of them ended its days in Imperial Airways livery, in October 1932, having in ten years flown half a million miles in 5,473hr.

Handley Page developed the design further into the triple-engined Hampstead which gained favour with Imperial Airways who wanted to order five of them, in November 1925. Delivery was so protracted that de Havilland was invited to tender and the DH66 Hercules was ordered to fly the Cairo-Basra route in January 1927. The Hampstead was the first of the Handley Page aircraft to conform with the ruling of the International Commission on Air Navigation that pilots should always sit on the left-hand side of the cockpit.

In 1925 Imperials found themselves short of multi-engined aircraft for the cross-Channel services. Rather than design a new aeroplane, Handley Page carried out a rush job in grafting the forward fuselage of a W8 to the Hyderabad bomber, the fuselage of which was fitted internally in a similar manner to the W8. This hybrid was designated W10 and first flown by Hubert Broad, from Cricklewood, on 10 February 1926. Four were built for Imperial Airways. In 1933, two of them were sold to Sir Alan Cobham, one to join his famous National Aviation Day display fleet, the other to be converted to the aerial tanker role with which he pioneered an effective system of in-flight refuelling.

These were the last of the O/400 derivatives which served the airlines for 16 years during the critical formative years of British civil aviation. Illustrated are **15** two W8Bs and **16** the interior of a W10. *Flight (both)*

landed in similar fashion in front of the maintenance hangar.

Imperial Airways soon realised that for the long distance routes to the Far East flying boats were likely to be the best solution as their landing areas were ready

made with only minimal shore facilities being required. So, in February 1928 from the works of Short Brothers at Rochester was launched the prototype of the Calcutta class boats powered by three Bristol Jupiter engines. Carrying 15 passengers, they entered service on the Mediterranean routes on 31 March 1929.

Whilst Croydon represented the peak of air traffic handling and navigation in Europe, it must not be forgotten that, by 1927, the Americans were operating 13 long distance air-mail routes with powerful beacons every few miles. With its network of efficient, fast and comfortable railroads, the United States had no incentive to develop passenger airlines with contemporary aircraft which were hardly any faster than trains, but with a much lower standard of safety and comfort.

Air mail, however, was a different matter. Smaller, faster aeroplanes with 'press-on-regardless' pilots could show considerable savings in time provided they survived the hazards of the operation — hazards which would be quite intolerable on a passenger route. So, in 1925, the Kelly Air Mail Act was passed to permit private operators to carry the mail on regular scheduled services.

Croydon in the 1920s

17
The sign at the entrance.

18
The 1928 harvest is brought in near Plough Lane. In the background is the Air Union hangar and Le021 airliners.

19
A drawing by G. H. Davis for the *Illustrated London News* of the new Croydon Airport traffic control system in 1929.
London Borough of Sutton Public Library (all)

20, 21
The Armstrong Whitworth Argosy, the company's first civil aircraft and its interior. First flown in March 1926, the Argosy was already outdated by the contemporary monoplanes of Fokker and Junkers: nevertheless, the standard of comfort and safety inherent in this very conservative design ensured it a highly competitive position in the European airline network.

The fuselage was of steel tube construction, covered with fabric, outboard of the centre section, the wings were wooden structures. With three 410hp Armstrong Siddeley Jaguar engines the Argosy II carried up to 28 passengers at a cruising speed of 95mph. The range was 520 miles. In May 1927 Imperial Airways inaugurated the famous 'Silver Wing' service on the London-Paris route with the Argosy I. On the mid-day flight a superb lunch was served by the steward. It became a tradition with the national airline and provided excellent copy for the travel writers. Seven Argosys were built.
British Airways (both)

Chief pilot of Robertson Aircraft Corporation of Missouri, holder of the second mail contract issued, was Charles A. Lindbergh. On 15 April 1926, he took off in a de Havilland DH4 to fly a bag of mail from Chicago to St Louis, later that day, he and two other pilots flew three loads of mail from St Louis to Chicago.

Thus began the great American airline tradition and the first mail operations of a company which, in 1929, was to become a part of the Aviation Corporation which was set up to purchase companies involved in aviation. Other air routes were opened up by the corporation which ultimately became American Airlines.

In 1927 Juan Terry Trippe, a 28-year old World War 1 naval pilot, founded a new airline in the belief that oceans were for flying over as well as for sailing on. With a fleet of two Fokker FVII trimotor aircraft, 24 employees and a contract to fly the mail between Key West, Florida and Havana in Cuba he commenced operations on 28 October 1927. In 1928 he carried more than 1,100 passengers and increased the fleet to seven aircraft.

Charles Lindbergh joined him and surveyed other routes to islands in the Caribbean, Mexico and Central and South America. In this modest way Pan American World Airways was born. Before many of the new routes could be opened up, new bases had to be created, often being hacked out of jungle clearings. By the end of 1929 Pan Am was a major international airline with a 12,000-mile route system linking 23 countries. New longer-range aircraft were built to Trippe's specification. Some were specialised aircraft to serve areas where land bases were impossible. One such machine was the Sikorsky S38 amphibian which was said to 'carry its own airport on its bottom'. It was the forerunner of a line of Sikorsky flying boats which set high standards of safety, reliability and comfort on Pan Am's over-water routes throughout the 1930s.

Another famous American airline developed from a crop-dusting purge of the boll weevil which threatened the Louisiana cotton crop in 1924. Delta Air Service developed into one of the major carriers, Delta Air Lines.

Further north, in Canada, commercial aviation was confined mainly to bush flying, with prospectors attempting to exploit the vast mineral wealth of the country. By 1929 there were 81 companies

22
First flown on 30 September 1926, the de Havilland DH66 Hercules was designed for the mail route from Croydon to Karachi which Imperial Airways took over from the RAF as a result of the 1925 Agreement with the Air Ministry. It carried up to 14 passengers if the mail load was reduced accordingly. It was also used by West Australian Airways. With three 450hp Bristol Jupiter radial engines, it cruised at 110mph and a range of 525 miles was claimed in de Havilland advertising, which also quoted a press report: 'Maximum comfort for the passengers combined with really high performance and the embodiment of every safety precaution render it the finest and most up-to-date commercial aircraft in the world'. Eleven were built.
British Aerospace Hatfield

23
The Sikorsky S40 flying boat — only three of these flying boats were built for Pan American but they set up a remarkable record of punctuality and safety. In two years they made over 1,000 flights, with 99% of them arriving on time. First flown in 1931, the S40 carried up to 32 passengers in a high degree of luxury. In 1934 the S40 was joined by the very handsome S42 which is often quoted as the first true flying boat airliner developed in America. The sleek hull accommodated up to 32 passengers in considerable comfort. Its four 700hp Pratt & Whitney Hornet engines gave it a cruising speed of 170mph compared with its predecessor's 115mph; the range was increased from 900 to 1,200 miles. Ten S42s were built.
Pan American World Airways

23

One of Delta's first tickets from Monroe, Louisiana to Jackson, Mississippi in 1929.

24
A 1929 advertisement showing Delta's route system and their Travelair monoplane. By 12 June 1930 it had been extended to Atlanta, Georgia. Presumably the reference to emergency landing fields was intended to encourage the prospective passenger!
Delta Airlines

25
One of Delta's first tickets from Monroe, Louisiana to Jackson, Mississippi in 1929.
Delta Airlines

26
A DH61, known as the 'Giant Moth', in service on the mail routes of Qantas. With a 500hp Bristol Jupiter engine it would carry six passengers at a cruising speed of 110mph. Range was 650 miles. Ten were built.

25

26

operating in this way. In 1931 several of them amalgamated to form Canadian Airways which ran an inter-city air mail service.

In the southern hemisphere two other pioneers, ex-wartime pilots Hudson Fysh and P. J. McGuinness, were conscious of the potential of air travel in the vast areas of their country with virtually no means of communication faster than a Model T Ford bouncing over a trackless wilderness. In November 1920 they registered a company in the imposing name of Queensland and Northern Territory Aerial Services Ltd, quickly abbreviated to QANTAS, the name by which this superb airline is known today.

Initially their 'fleet' of one BE2E and one Avro 504K war-surplus aircraft was used for joy-riding to convince the public that these 'new fangled' flying machines were safe. They carried 871 passengers over 34,000 miles without mishap.

On 2 November 1922 Hudson Fysh flew their Armstrong Whitworth FK8 over the second stage of their first scheduled route from Charleville to Cloncurry, a distance of 577 miles with an overnight stop at Longreach. Not until the early 1930s, however, did Qantas move forward to become one of the world's principal airlines. Qantas was building the de Havilland DH50 under licence and was interested in purchasing the eight seater Vickers Vulcan single-engined airliner, known as the 'flying pig', probably as much for its flying qualities as for its obese appearance. In negotiations with Vickers, Fysh stressed the very high ambient temperatures in which the aircraft would operate on the Charleville-Cloncurry route upon which it would be used, insisting that tropical radiators be fitted. There was much delay in shipping the Vulcan to Australia for evaluation, some of it was due to Vickers' inability to find a pilot who would sign Clause 8 of the Agreement — to abstain from taking alcoholic liquor! Ultimately one was found with a controllable thirst, Capt Godfrey Wigglesworth, and the machine was shipped. Qantas had rejected it, prior to despatch, on the basis of unfavourable reports from England, but Vickers insisted upon a demonstration at their own expense.

On 27 March 1923 the Vulcan lumbered into Longreach where the whole of the town's population turned out to see it. Every member of the Qantas board also appeared, their confidence not exactly enhanced when they saw the pilot padding around in his carpet slippers! Nevertheless, realising that they must fly in it to show their confidence, the officials insisted that engine checks should be made before take-off. This particular pilot did not bother with such niceties and, regardless of wind direction, hurtled along the rough ground, just missing the boundary fence as the 'pig' staggered into the air, only managing to achieve an altitude of 500ft whilst the 'top brass' looked longingly at the ground, their field of vision in the banked turn, comprising Longreach hospital and the local cemetery! The heat and noise were overpowering and, after an hour in the air they were thankful to land and retire to the Longreach Club for a liquid convalescence!

The Vulcan was only marginally more successful in the temperate climes of Europe. It was underpowered and of the nine built, two were fitted with more powerful Napier Lion engines and went into service with Imperial Airways.

In November 1929 the world's largest airliner, and certainly one of the most remarkable aeroplanes built before the war, made its first flight from the Junkers airfield at Dessau. This was Hugo Junker's G38.

In 1919 Junkers had commenced work on JG1, a large four engined all metal, cantilever wing airliner to carry a crew of two and nine passengers. It followed the well-proved corrugated duralumin skin technique but the fuselage construction was quite novel. Three large-diameter tubes formed the main longerons of the triangular section, one at the base, the other two forming the top longerons. They were linked by curved frames with triangulated bracing within the frames.

Most of the passenger accommodation was planned to be within the deep wing centre section and a buffet was to be provided. The only windows were to be in the cabin roof, a scheme not likely to be received with enthusiasm by those incarcerated within.

In 1921 The Allied Control Commission decided that the almost completed JG1 must be destroyed. Undeterred, Hugo Junkers continued to design other remarkable aircraft, one, the J1000

planned in 1923/4, was a huge canard type airliner with the tailplane forward of the wing which had a span of 262ft. It was planned to carry a crew of 10 and 100 passengers. All the passenger accommodation was to be in the wings and two restaurants would be available to them during the 1½-day flight across the Atlantic. The four engines would be accessible for maintenance in flight, and a retractable undercarriage was to be fitted.

The aircraft remained on the drawing board as the G38 reached the design office in 1928. This was a much more realistic project. The wing span was 144ft and the structure comprised a multi-spar arrangement of six large diameter tubes concentrated in the thickest part of the section, with 12 secondary tubes, all braced by diagonal and vertical struts. The duralumin corrugated skin was riveted to the structural members.

The undercarriage was an impressive engineering job reminiscent of techniques used in the 1960s. The two main undercarriage wheels on each side were mounted between two massive aluminium alloy castings which were pivoted at the end of the shock absorbing leg. Four 12-cylinder Junkers L88 engines of 700hp each were installed, driving four-bladed propellers.

28
Designed by Rex Pierson and first flown in May 1922 the Vickers Vulcan was an attempt to build an airliner which would be economical to run without Government subsidy. The oval section plywood fuselage accommodated eight passengers, the pilot's cockpit being high on the nose. With one 360hp Rolls-Royce Eagle engine it was underpowered, cruising at 90mph with a range of 360 miles. Only nine were built. *Vickers*

29
Germany's jumbo of the 1930s, the Junkers G38 had a wing span of 144ft, length of 76ft and was 23ft 7in high. Its all-up weight was 52,900lb. The seats, for up to 34 passengers, were on two decks on the second version to be built, also in the leading edges of the wings and in a small nose cabin. Its four 750hp Junkers Jumo diesel engines gave it a cruising speed of 129mph and the range was 1,180 miles. A crew of six was carried. Only two were built, one of them being seen occasionally at Croydon from 1932. *Lufthansa*

In the wing centre section was an 11-seat cabin forward and another one aft. The passengers had to be content with roof windows. At the rear was a cabin for four people whilst the other four passengers had the good fortune to sit in two small cabins in the leading edge of the centre section, with large windows in front.

The prototype saw limited service on the prestige routes of Deutsche Luft Hansa from May 1931 and a second one was built with the passenger complement increased to 34 by deepening the fuselage and building a second level above the main cabin. This machine was impressed into the Luftwaffe on the outbreak of war. Six G38s were built under licence as bombers by the Japanese firm of Mitsubishi.

Another German colossus, contemporary

30,31
The Dornier DoX was an attempt to develop the design of the successful Wal to its maximum size and it was the largest aircraft in the world when it first flew in 1929. Span was 157ft 6in, length 131ft and height 31ft 6in to the top of the 12 propellers. Originally powered by 12 German-built Bristol Jupiter engines of 525hp each, it could only climb to 1,400ft, so 640hp Curtiss Conqueror units were fitted, as shown in the photograph. The ceiling was only increased to 1,670ft, the reason probably being the inefficiency of the stubby wing, highly loaded, with its efficiency being reduced by interference of the vital upper surface airflow by the massive engine mountings. The maximum speed was 134mph and the range 1,740 miles. Only three were built.
Lufthansa (both)

30

with the G38, was the Dornier DoX flying boat. Designed to carry up to 170 passengers — although 100 proved to be its service maximum — over sectors of the trans-Atlantic route, it set up a world record on a test flight in October 1929 by carrying 169 people on a one-hour flight — nine of them were stowaways!

The DoX left Lake Constance for New York on 2 November 1930, flying via Amsterdam, Calshot, Lisbon and the Canary Isles. There were many problems en route, from storms to fire on board. The aircraft arrived at New York on 5 August 1931.

At this time the German passenger airships had been setting high standards of reliability and comfort on world air routes for several years. Junkers and Dornier were determined to compete with the dirigible but the technology of the period was inadequate to permit the successful development of an aeroplane with the range of an airship.

Nevertheless, these great pioneering ventures laid the foundations for the solid achievements in later decades. What had already been proved to the aircraft manufacturers was the clear fact that the burgeoning civil air transport industry was one which would justify considerable expenditure on design and development of aeroplanes to meet the needs of the new airlines.

Growth of the Airlines

1930 saw civil aviation well established throughout the world. Airports, many of them based upon the Croydon pattern, were being built to serve the capital cities which had not, hitherto, been on the air routes. The existence of these airports and the growth in air transport, which had become quite spectacular, found Deutsche Luft Hansa setting a cracking pace which outstripped all its contempories in Europe having carried 58,000 passengers since it began operations. DLH's close rival was the Dutch airline, Koninklijke Luchvaart Maatschappij NV-KLM, Royal Dutch Airlines, the 'Royal' being an unprecedented honour conferred, by Queen Wilhelmina, upon the new company before it was officially founded on 7 October 1919 by Albert Plesman, a talented young lieutenant in the Dutch Army Air Arm; he was its inspiration and guiding spirit until he died in 1953.

The close co-operation between Antony Fokker and Albert Plesman benefited both companies and was a powerful element in the rapid progress made by both KLM and Fokker. By 1930, 65% of the world's transport aircraft had been built by Fokker, and the reliability of his products soon permitted KLM to fly, in October 1924, an FVII from Amsterdam to the Dutch East Indies, 9,553 miles away. A regular service began five years later.

Fokker's famous range of high wing cantilever monoplanes, of mixed wood and metal construction, culminated in the graceful four-engined FXXXVI, which first flew in 1934. By this time it had been eclipsed by Donald Douglas's classic, the all-metal DC-1.

In other European countries airlines were becoming an important element of the commercial scene. France and Italy were well up in the pecking order. Italy having carried 40,000 passengers by 1930. The Italian airline, Ala Littoria, formed by the amalgamation of two smaller ones, began to operate the Savoia Marchetti S55 twin-hull flying boat of very distinctive and original design.

The S66 boat followed but, as airports were developed, Savoia Marchetti turned its design talents towards landplanes, developing a series of multi-engined, cantilever wing transports of mixed wood and metal construction, as were most of the transport aircraft of the period. In 1932 the S71 trimotor high wing monoplane appeared, with a distinctly Fokker lineage. It was followed by the outstanding S73 in 1934. Sabena, the Belgian airline, was the first to put the S73 into service in Europe in 1935, to replace the ageing Fokker FVII3Ms.

Surprisingly, the Soviet Union had moved rapidly after 1923 when a state-subsidised line, called Dobrolet, was established to serve the whole of the USSR. From 1928 to 1932 67,000 passengers and 5,900 tons of freight and mail had been carried in the Russian-built Tupolev ANT-9s and other aircraft purchased in Europe. In 1932 the state airline was renamed Aeroflot and more indigenous designs were introduced into the fleet.

In Poland, Spain, Rumania, Scandinavia and Switzerland airlines were operating. In

32
The White Star liner 'Homeric' was the official ship for the 1931 Schneider Trophy Race. Seen on board are Antony Fokker and Frederick Handley Page. *Richard T. Riding*

33,34
The 108ft span Fokker FXXXVI
was their first, and only, four-
engined aircraft. Although of
traditional mixed construction,
the slab-sided appearance
disappeared and an elegant
shape resulted in an efficient
airliner which carried 32
passengers and a crew of four
in considerable comfort
cruising at 149mph over a range
of 839 miles. It had four 750hp
Wright Cyclone engines. Only
one was built out of six ordered
by KLM for their Far Eastern
routes. Five were cancelled in
favour of operating the DC-2.
KLM

35
Savoia Marchetti S55 flying
boat was developed from a
military machine which
achieved prominence in 1933
when General Balbo led a
formation of 24 in a flight from
Italy to the Chicago World Fair.
The commercial version was in
service on the Mediterranean
routes from 1926 to 1937. The
hulls were of wooden
construction, the tail unit being
carried on braced booms whilst
the thick wooden wing had a
covered cockpit near the
leading edge. This design led to
the S66 with three 750hp Fiat
engines driving pusher
propellers. The S66 is
illustrated. *John Stroud*

March 1931 the early Swiss lines Belair and Ad Astra merged to form Swissair and continued to operate their Junkers and Fokker machines.

After a late start, the growth of civil aviation in the United States had been so swift that, by 1930, 40 small airlines, owning 500 aircraft between them, flew a route system 31,000 miles long. In 1928, 60,000 passengers had been carried; in the following year the total rose to 160,000, an increase of 50,000 on the number carried by the German lines, which were pre-eminent in Europe.

Boeing, Douglas, Lockheed (or Loughead, as they were known originally), and Sikorsky were the design leaders in America with other smaller manufacturers such as Stinson, Bellanca, Curtiss, Ryan and the little known Clark company producing innovative designs for which only a limited market emerged.

Lockheed had made a major impression on the airlines in 1927 with the Vega radial-engined high wing monoplane. It was designed for an air race from California to Hawaii. Sadly, it crashed into the Pacific Ocean during the race but had proved so promising that a second one was built as a demonstrator. Beautifully streamlined, this five-seater machine was one of the earliest examples of a moulded plywood monocoque fuselage with no internal bracing, all the stresses being taken by the shell itself. With a top speed of 145mph on a modest 220hp from the Wright J6 engine, the prototype set up a record speed from Los Angeles to Oakland, California on its first flight. From the Vega, Hall Hibberd developed the Orion, very similar in appearance, but fitted with a retractable undercarriage.

Lockheed's arch rival, Bill Boeing, had formed the Boeing Airplane Company on 26 April 1917. He built other firm's designs under Government contract and, in March 1919, opened an air mail service between America and Canada. He won a contract for an Army 'pursuit ship', as the Americans called fighters in those days and this produced a steady income for the company enabling him to return to this first love, civil aviation.

The DH4 was widely used in the US Mail Service so in 1926 Boeing built a replacement, the Model 40 biplane, with a Pratt and Whitney Wasp engine. In addition to the mail it would carry two

passengers in a cramped cabin to return an extra $400 of revenue on a flight from San Francisco to Chicago. As this particular route was open for tender he bid successfully for it. He founded Boeing Air Transport in 1927 and built 81 Model 40A transports and 40 Model 40Bs with more powerful engines. These aircraft carried out a major job in pioneering airline operations in the States and they convinced Bill Boeing that a larger machine was necessary. He swiftly designed and put into production the famous Model 80.

In 1930 he made another dramatic leap forward. Fokker's monoplanes were popular in America, and Boeing made a study of his methods, particularly the new technique of welding steel tubes by means of an electric arc. He decided to build an all metal, stressed skin, cantilever low-wing

36
A mechanic starting the starboard engine of a Swissair Fokker FVIIB in 1931. Note the decorative treatment of the unpainted aluminium sections of the engine cowlings and undercarriage oleo leg, small, overlapping whorls produced, usually, by an apprentice rotating a piece of emery cloth on the end of his thumb!
Swissair

37
Designed by Jack Northrop, later to start his own aircraft company, the Lockheed Orion was one of the cleanest aeroplanes built in the 1930s. It was also one of the fastest with a top speed of 225mph in its production form, powered by a 420hp Pratt & Whitney engine. This machine was operated by Swissair. *Swissair*

38
Cabin interior of a Boeing 247. Comparison with the DC-2 interior shows the more spacious layout of the Douglas machine with luggage stowage racks instead of nets. Note the spring clips for hats on the cabin walls. Powered by two 550hp Pratt & Whitney Wasp engines the Boeing 247 was a giant stride forward in air transport. Based on the Monomail and a bomber design, Boeing used metal for the whole of the structure, the fuselage being a semi-monocoque structure. Long chord cowlings, to reduce drag, enclosed the engines which drove three-blade fixed pitch propellers, which, in the 247D model, became controllable pitch units. The undercarriage was retractable. A cruising speed of 155mph was achieved with 10 passengers, a crew of three and a range of 485 miles.
Boeing Company Archives

39
A Ford Trimotor of American Airways. Henry Ford realised the immense impact the Fokker FVII designs were having in the aviation industry so, in 1925, he bought the Stout Metal Airplane Company. The Ford Trimotor was the first machine to be built under the new management. Known as the 'Tin Goose', it was a very simple aeroplane, embracing Bill Stout's philosophy that 'What I don't fit in my aeroplanes don't give no trouble'! 194 were built between June 1926 and June 1933 and played a major part in developing the US airline network. With three Wright Whirlwind engines of 300hp it carried up to 11 passengers, cruising at 107mph.
American Airlines

monoplane as a mail carrier and then increased the length of the fuselage to accommodate eight passengers. It had a 575hp Pratt and Whitney Hornet radial engine and a retractable undercarriage. A speed of 158mph was achieved, the performance being degraded by the absence of a variable pitch propeller. Boeing had to be content with a fixed pitch wooden one with a blade angle which gave a compromise between take-off and top speed.

The Monomail, as the new aircraft was called, showed such a remarkable improvement in technology and performance that it was decided to build a twin-engined machine based upon it. The outcome was the Boeing 247, one of the most significant aircraft in the saga of air transport.

It was originally intended to build it for United Airlines with a larger, wider fuselage, twin Hornet engines in Townend ring cowlings, variable pitch propellers and pneumatic de-icer boots along the leading edges of the wings and tail surfaces; the planned all-up weight being 16,000lb. When United's pilots saw the design and specification they rejected it out of hand, insisting that 12,000lb was the

40
The unusual paintwork of this American Airlines Douglas DC-2 gives it a curious plan view against a dark background. The effective compromise between the parallel lines of the passenger cabin — dictated by economical production methods, and the well streamlined nose, tail, nacelle and wing root fillet is evident. The DC-2 cruised at 198mph with 14 passengers. Range was 1,000 miles and 138 were built. *McDonald Douglas*

41
The interior of a Delta Airlines DC-2. With the introduction of the type in 1940, Delta recruited stewardesses for the first time. All the girls were registered nurses. *Delta Airlines*

42
The flight deck of a Douglas DC-2.
KLM Royal Dutch Airlines

43
Contemporary with the Boeing
247, and its strong competitor,
the Curtiss-Wright Condor
originated in 1928 as a
converted bomber. In 1932 the
T32 was designed with a
payload of 3,200lb powered by
two 750hp Wright Cyclone
engines. It also had a semi-
retractable undercarriage,
leaving the wheels partly
exposed to reduce damage in
the event of a belly landing. In
an attempt to overcome the
handicap of low speed by
comparison with the Douglas
and Boeing monoplanes the
type was offered as a sleeper to
carry 12 passengers. Condors
remained in scheduled services
in the USA until 1936.
American Airlines

44
Miss Nelly Diener, Swissair's
first air stewardess,
photographed in 1934 with a
Curtiss-Wright Condor
operating the Zurich-Berlin
service. *Swissair*

43

44

correct weight. By this short-sighted
attitude Boeing was forced into the trap
which many manufacturers — sadly, some
recent British ones — have experienced, of
designing an aeroplane for one customer,
only to find that no other wants it. United
ordered 59 247s and later bought 13 of the
247D version with more power, as the
original model had a marginal performance
operating out of hot and high airports.
Criticism was also levelled at the fact that
the wing spar was an obstruction in the
cabin.

In 1931 the United States Bureau of Air
Commerce issued a warning about airliners
with wooden spars and recommended
frequent inspection. This was expensive
and, in some cases, alarming.
Transcontinental and Western Air, TWA,
tried to buy the Boeing 247 but could not
take delivery until the United order had
been completed. It was decided by the
board that TWA would issue its own
specification to several companies for
design submissions to be made. The most
important requirement was that the
aircraft must be able to take off at full load
with one engine out, from any airport used
by the airline. It seemed, therefore, that as
the machine must carry at least 12
passengers a trimotor layout would be
required. Donald W. Douglas had 'cut his
teeth' since forming his company in July
1920, on a mixed bag of private owner and
small military aircraft. In 1923 he was
awarded a contract to build five machines
to fly round the world. The result was the
Douglas World Cruiser, two of which did,
indeed, achieve this feat under the control
of the Army Air Service. The flight took six
months and six days. The company logo
was immediately redesigned as a globe
with the words 'First around the world'
upon it.

When the TWA enquiry reached Douglas
he arranged for a Ford Trimotor — the 'Tin
Goose', as it was known — to be flown to
his airfield at Santa Monica for inspection.

It was decided that it would not be difficult to improve on this metal derivative of Fokker's designs. He considered that, by very careful attention to streamlining and weight control, an advanced airliner could be produced which had none of the disadvantages of the Boeing 247, and would offer superior cabin accommodation and a very high performance on two engines.

On 1 July 1933 the Douglas DC-1 flew for the first time. A new breed of airliner had arrived. It was of all metal, stressed skin construction and, with its successors, the DC-2 and DC-3, was the brainchild of Donald Douglas, and Bailey Oswald. The undercarriage was retractable. The roomy 12-seat cabin was unobstructed by the multi-cellular wing structure which was underneath the floor. Some minor modifications were made and more powerful engines fitted. TWA ordered 20 of the type which, in its production form, became the DC-2 with a longer fuselage accommodating 14 passengers. 710hp Cyclone engines were installed, driving three-bladed, controllable pitch metal propellers which enabled the pilot to select the blade angle appropriate to the needs of the aeroplane during the flight. Clean-lined aircraft such as the Boeing 247 and the DC-2 tended to 'float' across the aerodrome as they landed, so Donald Douglas introduced split flaps at the trailing edge of the wing to overcome this. Icing problems were a serious handicap to all-weather flying until the advent of the gas turbine offered large volumes of heated air which could be ducted through the leading edges of wings. A deicing paste smeared over the surfaces had limited effect, but Douglas fitted Goodyear rubber deicing boots along the wing and tail surfaces of the DC-2. These were pulsated by air pressure to break up the ice as it formed. Even these were quite inadequate on occasions. Ernest K. Gann, himself an airline pilot before the war, tells in his book *Fate is the Hunter* of a night flight in a DC-2 from Nashville, Tennessee to New York. At an altitude sufficiently high to clear the Blue Ridge Mountains, the aircraft flew into severe icing conditions. Initially the boots controlled the ice accretion but soon they were overpowered and could be seen pulsating beneath the rapidly developing ice layer which began to have a very serious effect upon the lifting capacity of the wing. The rudder froze and power was lost due to carburettor icing, whilst the side of the cockpit was bombarded with chunks of ice hurled off the propeller blades, in spite of the the glycol spray from the root which was intended to keep each blade free of ice.

After an appallingly dangerous flight with the wings still loaded with ice, and for much of the time being unable to contract radio direction finding stations to establish their position, Gann's captain landed safely at Cincinnati with the windscreen almost opaque through ice layers.

This vivid account reveals the major problem facing aircraft designers, pilots and operators in the 1930s when the technology of the various aspects of aircraft design and operation was out of step in a number of important areas. Nevertheless, the Americans had learned the hard way, particularly from the Mail pilots, who pressed on regardless until 1934, when President Roosevelt decided that the Mail Contracts had been negotiated by the Post Master General of the previous administration on the basis of collusion and fraud.

General Ben D. Foulis, the Chief of the US Army Air Corps, was instructed to take over all mail operations from the civil contractors. Foulis thought it would be good practice for his pilots in spite of their lack of any real experience of night flying by instruments.

After a disastrous six weeks on the mail

45
Their expressions suggesting deep unhappiness, this group posed in the passenger accommodation of the Airship R100, includes Nevil Shute Norway on the stair. The oriental rug and wicker chairs contrast with the stark functional design of the structure. The creased tablecloth reflects little credit upon the steward! *Vickers*

45

A. Hessell Tiltman BSc, CEng, FRAeS

46
Hessell Tiltman was a superb craftsman and an original thinker whose ideas, such as the retractable undercarriage in 1933 and fireproof fuel tanks in 1939, met with much opposition and prejudice. With N. S. Norway, better known as Nevil Shute, he worked with Geoffrey de Havilland, and later, with Barnes Wallis, on the R100 airship, starting Airspeed in a York bus garage in 1931.

With the retractable undercarriage, his greatest contribution to British aviation was the introduction of a photographic technique which enabled the lines of the largest aeroplane to be laid out full scale on special tables. Photolofting led to considerable savings in production time and higher standards of interchangeability of components — vital considerations for wartime production. The author was privileged to enjoy his friendship in his later years and remains convinced that this modest man, as with his successor at Airspeed, Arthur Hagg, did not receive the recognition due to him.

46

47
Airspeed Ferry under construction in the York bus garage in 1931. A Tern glider fuselage is suspended from the roof. *Airspeed Ltd*

47

routes which cost the lives of 12 pilots in 60 crashes, the operation reverted to the civilian operators — and the charges of collusion and fraud were later admitted to be totally unjustified.

The airlines were impressed with the DC-2 which was ordered by American Airlines, Eastern Air Lines, and in Europe, by KLM and Swissair. The passengers liked it as they no longer had to walk down the cabin in a stooping posture. 138 were built before a further development, the DC-3, introduced what is probably the greatest transport aeroplane ever produced, and one for which the aircraft industries of the world have tried, mostly unsuccessfully, until the present day, to build a true replacement.

Returning to Britain, we find a much less satisfactory situation. The substantial market which has always existed in America for its own aeroplanes had no parallel in this country — such a situation still obtains. So, whilst American manufacturers were sufficiently enterprising, and could afford to tool up for quantity production of the complex all-metal aircraft which were going into service, British manufacturers were tending to keep to wooden construction or to build simple metal aeroplanes on a 'knife

and fork' basis. They had an additional burden in that the monoplane configuration was still frowned upon in official circles, this being a legacy of events going back to before the Great War when a number of monoplanes, inadequate in strength, crashed with fatal consequences after disintegration in the air.

In 1932 the small firm of Airspeed Limited decided to build a very advanced low wing cantilever monoplane. Airspeed grew out of the disastrous end, on 4 October 1930, of Britain's leviathan of the air, the 777ft-long airship R101 built at the Government Airship Works at Cardington, Bedfordshire, in competition with the Vickers-built R100, designed by that great engineer, Barnes Wallis, and constructed at Howden in Yorkshire.

On the Howden staff were Nevil Shute Norway and Alfred Hessell Tiltman, very competent de Havilland-trained engineers, who viewed with dismay the ill-conceived flight of their rival to India before it had been thoroughly tested. A few hours after leaving Cardington, R101 crashed at Beauvais, in Northern France, most of the crew and passengers dying in the holocaust.

R100, which had already proved itself in a flight to Canada, and was considered to

48
Airspeed AS4 Ferry prototype in flight. Note the well glazed cockpit to give the best possible visibility for the pilot when orbiting aerodromes at low level during air displays. As far as possible control runs were located outside the structure for easy maintenance. Three de Havilland Gipsy engines of 120hp each enabled 10 passengers to be flown at a cruising speed of 100mph. It was a very simple and reliable machine which, it was hoped, would appeal to other operators. Only four were built — the cheaper and faster de Havilland DH84 Dragon was much more attractive. *BAe*

49
Airspeed's elegant Envoy was flown for the first time by Flt Lt C. H. A. Colman on 26 June 1934. Fitted with two Wolseley AR9 200hp engines, it had a cruising speed of 150mph and a range of 403 miles. More powerful engines and wing flaps were fitted to later versions.

Of all wooden construction this shapely aeroplane reveals the artistry of its designer, A. Hessell Tiltman. The prototype was shown at the Society of British Aircraft Constructors Show at Hendon on 2 July 1934 and created a sensation by comparison with the collection of primitive RAF biplanes on show; not even the fighters were fitted with retractable undercarriages, and the twin engined bombers were all slower than the Envoy. Over 80 were built. *BAe*

50
Sir Alan Cobham's Airspeed Courier being refuelled in the air from a Handley-Page W10 tanker. Note the co-pilot, Sqn Ldr W. Helmore, standing with his shoulders out of the cabin, to release the hose after completion of fuel transfer.

be in the *Graf Zeppelin* class, was immediately scrapped, and the development of rigid airships was terminated in Britain.

Norway and Tiltman started Airspeed in a York bus garage with a modest capital of £6,300. Their first venture was the Tern, a high performance sailplane, followed by an unusual machine for Sir Alan Cobham, who was on their board, and was planning his famous National Air Day Displays which in the 1930s introduced many thousands of people to flying. He required a small

51
The Lockheed 10A Electra was the company's first venture into all-metal construction. It was powered by two 450hp Pratt & Whitney Wasp Junior engines, other similar engines were optional. British Airways operated five Electras, each carrying 10 passengers and two pilots at a cruising speed of 195mph. The fuselage was a metal monocoque whilst the wing construction was unusual with a corrugated metal interior and a smooth external skin, a rather complicated technique to achieve torsional strength. 148 Electras were built. *BA*

52
The interior of a British Airways Electra showing the roominess and comfort of the cabin. The reclining chairs were adjustable and had a footrest. Overhead ventilation ducts and reading lights at the side of the seats were under the individual control of the passengers. *BA*

12-seat airliner for joyriding, so Tiltman designed the Ferry with three engines and the lower wing cranked downwards from the top of the fuselage to give a good view for all the passengers. It was not a commercial success for Airspeed although it served Cobham well.

Sir Alan was interested in refuelling aircraft in the air and he decided to develop the technique preparatory to making a flight to Australia without refuelling stops on the ground. He placed an order with Airspeed for a suitable machine which also had to have appeal to commercial operators.

Tiltman was faced with the classic problem of all aircraft designers — how to reconcile two almost irreconcilable design requirements! A long range aircraft, almost a flying petrol tank, with fuel capacity as far aft as possible, and a cabin machine seating six passengers as far forward as possible.

The AS4 Courier was an elegant solution to the equation. It was a cantilever low wing monoplane with a 240hp Lynx radial engine in a Townend ring cowling. An innovation was its retractable undercarriage, the first to be fitted to a British commercial aeroplane. The chairman of the company, Lord Grimthorpe, had been warned by an eminent designer of military aircraft to avoid the retractable wheels on the grounds that the system would be expensive, unreliable, heavy and have little effect upon performance. The Courier had a top speed of 163mph; with the undercarriage lowered, the speed dropped by 37mph.

Extended trials of the AS4 at the Aeroplane and Armament Experimental Establishment, Martlesham created a minor sensation at the Air Ministry. A demonstration was arranged before leading British aircraft designers. Norway

saw this as an exercise in 'rubbing their noses in it'. It is significant, however, that, from that time, all British high performance aeroplanes had retractable undercarriages.

The structure of the Courier was orthodox. The wooden fuselage was skinned in stress-bearing plywood and covered with doped fabric. The RAE was in a dilemma over the wings which had two spars with ribs and a stressed plywood skin; they were bolted to the centre section, which carried the undercarriage assemblies, the wheels being arranged to take the weight of the aircraft in the event of a landing with wheels up. There was very little experience of cantilever wings to draw upon, and it was not easy to determine whether the deflection of the wing by flight loads would impose the essential similar deflection upon both spars. The influence of the retractable undercarriage upon stress levels was

another imponderable at that time.

Finally the RAE sent a team and a lorryload of sandbags to York to proof-load the wings and measure the deflections under simulated flight conditions. The wing passed the tests.

The very clean lines of the Courier were characteristic of Tiltman's artistry. C. G. Grey, in *The Aeroplane*, commented, 'One of the best looking jobs I have ever seen . . . the latest Cellon finish on the Courier, which is done in dark and pale blue with scarlet lettering, can be put up against any multiple coated, hand polished and varnished American aeroplane that has ever been seen . . . Messrs Norway and Tiltman, in spite of being slide rule experts and practical engineers, are inherently artists . . . they seem to have the unusual faculty of being able to see the spray! Everything on the machine is faired off in the right way.'

Grey's perceptive remark about 'seeing

53
The de Havilland DH84 Dragon I differed visually from the Mk II in that the former had long cabin windows and an un-faired undercarriage. The fuselage, to which both upper and lower wings were attached, was a ply covered wooden box structure covered with doped fabric. Between 6 and 10 passengers could be accommodated. Two 130hp Gipsy Major engines gave the Mk II a cruising speed of 114mph, and a range of 545 miles. 202 of both types were built, of which 87 were produced by de Havilland, Australia. Its simple maintenance requirements and ability to operate from small fields ensured its success. *BAe*

54
The de Havilland 86 prototype housed a single pilot in the well glazed 'flight deck'. Later, at the request of Imperial Airways, it was enlarged to carry two pilots in a more shapely nose. Control problems were investigated at the Aeroplane and Armament Experimental Establishment at Martlesham, where aeroplanes underwent their Certificate of Airworthiness trials. As a result, small fins were added to the tips of the tailplane, the modified aircraft being known as the DH86B. Four 205hp Gipsy Six engines achieved a cruising speed of 145mph with 12 passengers. 62 Express Airliners were built, some served with Qantas, Imperial Airways and Jersey Airways; other important operators were Railway Air Services, formed by the four main British railway companies and Imperial Airways. In 1935 Hillman, Spartan, United and British Continental Airways merged to form British Airways. This line also operated the 86B.

Here a DH86B operated by the Croydon charter firm of Wrightwings Ltd is illustrated. *BAe*

55
The Armstrong Whitworth XV Atalanta was Britain's first monoplane airliner. Careful wind tunnel testing achieved a well streamlined form but, to the surprise of the designers, the ingenious undercarriage, with the shock absorbing struts inside the fuselage, created 25% of the fuselage drag. The main structure of the Atalanta was metal and wood, the cabin section being clad in plywood, whilst the after part was fabric covered, the form at the fuselage corners being achieved by curved aluminium fairings. Four 375hp Armstrong Siddeley Serval radial engines gave the Atalanta a cruising speed of 118mph with nine passengers in the spacious cabin. The range was 485 miles. Eight were built, some continuing to fly until the early 1940s. *BA*

56

the spray' pinpoints the difference between a good engineering designer who can produce a sound, but probably undistinguished aeroplane, and one with a highly developed aesthetic sense and the ability to analyse, at the drawing board stage, the finer points of airflow over the structure. Among the British designers with such talents in full measure were Arthur Hagg, later Airspeed's chief designer but at de Havilland in the 1930s; his successor at DH, R. E. Bishop; Dr A. E. Russell, now Sir Archibald, of the Bristol Aeroplane Company; Sydney Camm at Hawkers, and of course, the redoubtable

Edgar Percival. All of them produced beautiful and efficient aeroplanes in the days before computers and multi-national design teams of complete anonymity took over responsibility.

The Courier was undoubtedly a major achievement for this small company which moved to Portsmouth before the first flight. A twin-engined development of it, the handsome Envoy, appeared in 1934 and formed the basis of the finest twin-engined trainer of World War 2, the Oxford.

For all its design talent, Airspeed lacked

55

the marketing facilities which its rivals, de Havilland, possessed on a worldwide basis. In November 1932 the DH84 Dragon had been flown from Stag Lane aerodrome for the first time. The rough and tough Romford coach operator Edward Hillman unjustifiably claimed credit for the initiation of this design which was already under consideration as a submission for the Iraqi Air Force, who needed a twin-engined multi-purpose aircraft. Hillman saw it when he visited Stag Lane after his rejection of the Ferry. He ordered four Dragons at a price of £2,800 each, £1,175 less than the Ferry. With its two DH Gipsy

Major engines its running costs per ton/mile were less than the single Gipsy engined Fox Moth operated by Hillman. He intended to use the Dragon on the Paris route and undercut fares on Imperial Airways routes by one third. The Dragon was a most successful aeroplane backed by the powerful DH product back-up organisation.

In the early 1930s Arthur Hagg designed several significant de Havilland machines for the private owner. The DH85 Leopard Moth was an attractive three-seat successor to the earlier DH80 Puss Moth which suffered several fatal accidents when wings broke off in the air. The forward wing fixing point coincided with the location of the main shock absorbing strut of the undercarriage and it was thought that heavy landings might have weakened the structure, so on the Leopard Moth Hagg moved the strut fixing to the engine bearer location point. He also changed the construction of the fuselage from welded steel to a ply-covered box as in the Dragon, improving the ratio of structural to all-up weight sufficiently to enable a third passenger seat to be fitted.

Imperial Airways was forbidden by its charter to operate foreign aircraft. In

56
First flown in April 1934, the elegant de Havilland DH89 Dragon Rapide biplane, of classic line, was a refined version of the Dragon with two 200hp Gipsy Six engines. Appearance was greatly improved by graceful tapered wings which replaced the DH60 Moth wings used as outer panels on the Dragon. A trousered undercarriage and framed windows, as in the Mk II Dragon, were distinctive features. The DH89A had flaps on the lower wings. The Rapide carried six to eight passengers and could maintain height on one engine. 685 were built, many of them as 'Dominie' radio and navigational trainers during the war. Afterwards 18 of them formed BEA's 'Islander' class on the Channel, Scilly and Western Isles routes. *BAe*

57
Instrument panel of the Armstrong Whitworth XV Atalanta. *BA*

57

58
The drawing shows how the
characteristic tail design of
de Havilland and Airspeed
aircraft was perpetuated over a
number of years in different
aircraft.

59
The Short Kent flying boat was
developed from the 1927
Calcutta. The first flying boat
with a stressed skin metal hull
to go into commercial service,
the luxurious Kent had four
550hp Bristol Jupiter engines,
carried 16 passengers, cruised
at 105mph and had a range of
450 miles. Here *Sylvanus* is
seen over the Medway.
Short Bros Ltd

collaboration with Qantas, the Singapore-
Australia sector of the Britain to Australia
air route was to be developed. De Havilland
was invited to tender for a multi-engined
10-passenger aircraft for this sector, but
the fact that it must be designed, built and
certificated as airworthy by 31 January
1934 — four months later — presented a
serious problem.

Hagg designed the DH86 on the same
structural principles as the well-proven
Dragon but the lines were refined
considerably — the origins of the shape of
the later Dragon Rapide can be seen in the
Express Air Liner, as the DH86 was known.
Generally, highly tapered wings tend
towards unpleasant stalling
characteristics, and, although Hubert
Broad's test flying programme and indeed,
the Aircraft and Armament Experimental
Establishment's Certificate of
Airworthiness tests proceeded without
undue incident, a number of DH86s were
lost through control problems, including
one of the Qantas machines on its delivery
flight.

The structure of the fuselage was, in
effect, that of the Dragon turned inside out.
The interior was of stressed plywood
whilst the spruce longerons, struts and
stringers were outside it. The fabric
covering over the stringers faired the
fuselage to an attractive streamline shape
with the characteristic de Havilland tail
unit, which, in profile, had hardly changed
since the DH60 Moth in 1925.

It will be seen that a tremendous spirit of
optimism was apparent in civil aviation
circles but unfortunately, as Airspeed and
other smaller companies found to their
cost, many small airlines were being
formed with little but optimism to sustain
them. Aeroplanes were obtained on hire-
purchase agreements and within a few
months the manufacturer had to repossess
second-hand machines with little chance of
re-sale at a profitable price. The formation
of the three large British airline groups led
to a healthier home market for the
aeroplane builders.

In 1932 Imperial Airways had taken
delivery of the new Armstrong Whitworth
AWXV Atalanta. The first four-engined
monoplane to go into service with the line
was a complete breakaway from previous
AW technology as exemplified by the
venerable Argosy. It was required to fly the
route from Kenya to Cape Town, and
therefore, had to have the ability to fly
safely from hot and high aerodromes and,
be able to maintain a height of 9,000ft with
one engine out with a payload of 3,000lb.
John Lloyd, AW's chief designer, decided
that the increased wing loading and
consequent higher landing speed inherent
in the monoplane formula, and the heavier
wing construction, would be balanced by
the much cleaner lines of the aeroplane and
the improved performance which could be
achieved. The whole concept of the
Atalanta was well ahead of current British
thinking and even today the design looks
modern.

In Europe the Handley Page 42s were
flying the Imperial Airways flag in their
sedate manner, looking more and more
incongruous as the sleek Swissair and KLM
Douglas DC-2s began to use Croydon. In
spite of the derisive remarks of competitors
about the 'seven old ladies in crinolines
and poke bonnets' they were comfortable
and safe with a splendid cuisine on the
Silver Wing prestige flight to Paris.
Sir Peter Masefield, addressing a public

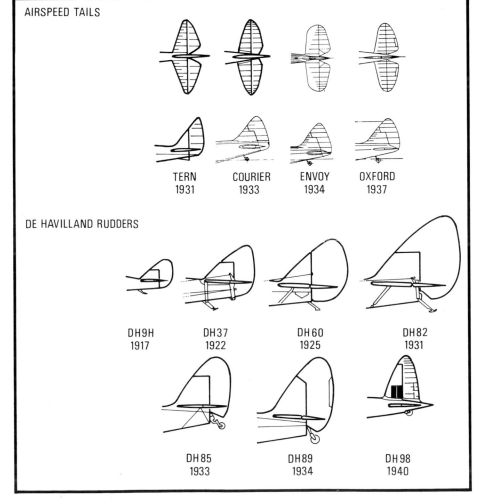

AIRSPEED TAILS

TERN 1931 · COURIER 1933 · ENVOY 1934 · OXFORD 1937

DE HAVILLAND RUDDERS

DH9H 1917 · DH37 1922 · DH60 1925 · DH82 1931

DH85 1933 · DH89 1934 · DH98 1940

meeting when he was chief executive of British European Airways, was asked why Imperial Airways, in the days of the old HP42, could always be relied upon to make a profit but with its new aircraft BEA made a loss. Sir Peter commented that 'The 42s were so slow that all the profit was made en route, in the bar!'

Imperial Airways decided that two more machines were necessary, but Handley Page could not build two 42s at an economical price. Maj Mayo, the airline's technical consultant, suggested a compromise solution by building a set of Short Kent flying boat wings upon a new fuselage. This was agreed and Short Brothers produced, at Rochester, two of the ugliest aeroplanes ever to serve a British airline. So *Scylla* and *Syrinx* went into service carrying 38 passengers. Pilots and passengers disliked them — compromise on this scale in aviation rarely pays.

In 1933 the French Government initiated the formation of Air France by a merger of Air Union with a number of other small airlines. This produced a fleet of landplanes and flying boats of remarkable diversity from Fokker FVIIBs to the excellent Potez 620 and 621, derived from the Potez 54 bomber and capable of carrying 10 to 15 passengers at 175mph.

Lufthansa was operating the famous

Junkers 52/3m on many of its routes. This remarkable transport was a direct descendant of the F13, W33 and W34 work-horses which led first to the Ju52 single-engined cargo aircraft, which could be mounted on floats. The 52/3m was the last Junkers aeroplane to use a corrugated metal skin: it was fitted with many different types of engine and was used throughout the world. Even British Airways operated three of them for night

60
Cabin of a 'Kent' class flying boat of Imperial Airways, which operated five on its Middle East services. *BA*

61
Handley Page 42 *Hengist* at Croydon. With four 490hp Bristol Jupiter engines, driving four-bladed propellers, this legendary airliner carried up to 24 seats in Pullman car luxury at a cruising speed of 95mph. It had a range of 500 miles. Eight were built and during their service with Imperial Airways they flew 10 million miles without injuring a passenger.
London Borough of Sutton Libraries

62
The interior of the cabin of the HP42.
London Borough of Sutton Libraries

62

63

mail services. Almost 5,000 were built, and the type formed the mainstay of the German airborne forces and transport units during the war.

In the 1930s, Lufthansa was, of course, a clandestine embryo air force to spearhead the Nazi dream of world conquest. It was an excellent training ground for crews, and a useful reconnaissance unit as its aircraft visited airports throughout the world. Its purchasing policy reflected this status. So-called airliners, such as the Heinkel He111 and the Junkers Ju86 had narrow fuselages, designed to carry bombs, but with just enough room for passengers in acute discomfort. Diesel engines were an interesting innovation at this time although their reliability and economy was over-shadowed by a considerable weight penalty.

A profound shock was administered in 1934 to the British aircraft and airline industries. The MacRobertson Air Race from RAF Mildenhall to Melbourne was to start on 20 October; the prize money was £10,000 and a gold cup, presented by the Australian industrialist Sir Macpherson Robertson.

De Havilland, at Hatfield, was rushing to deliver the new Express airliner to Qantas; Dragons, Fox Moths and Tiger Moths filled all spaces on the production line so there seemed little chance of a DH entry as high speed and long range were the obvious requirements. The de Havilland board found it most irksome to be out of such an important race with its tremendous challenge and potential for commercially valuable publicity, not only for the company, but for Britain. Many board meetings and design conferences took place, finally, a solution emerged. Using

63
Originally fitted with four
595hp Bristol Jupiter engines,
two Short L17s were built in
1933/34. The second one,
Syrinx, was re-engined with
four 660hp Pegasus engines,
with little improvement in
performance. The machine
cruised at 105mph, with 38
passengers. *BA*

64
A Lufthansa Junkers Ju52/3M
at the Croydon terminal
building. The aircraft went into
service with the airline in 1933
and proved to be an extremely
reliable and rugged aeroplane.
Lufthansa

65
The interior of a Junkers
Ju52/3M operated by Sabena.
Sabena

Before the twin engine Heinkel 111 went into service, Heinkel had produced a remarkable mail plane which could carry four passengers. The He70 was a low wing monoplane powered by a 630hp BMW in-line engine and was fitted with a retractable undercarriage. Designed to the order of Deutsche Lufthansa to meet the competition of Swissair who had begun to operate the fast Lockheed Orion on the Zurich-Munich-Vienna route, this very handsome aircraft, with its elliptical wooden cantilever wing and superbly streamlined flush riveted metal fuselage, cruised at 189mph with a range of 621 miles, but, as a single engine aircraft, was not really suitable for scheduled passenger routes where the high touch-down speed made forced landings extremely hazardous. One of these machines was bought by Rolls-Royce as a flying test bed for their new Kestrel in-line engine. The engine was sent to the Rostock factory to be fitted and rumour has it that it was fitted into a Messerschmitt Bf109 fighter and a Junkers Ju87 dive bomber for trials before being installed in Rolls-Royce's aeroplane!. *Flight*

two of the new and promising six-cylinder Gipsy engines, a suitable machine could be built in the nine months before the race. If a suitable variable pitch propeller could be found, it could fly at 200mph over stage lengths of 2,600 miles. A French Ratier propeller with pneumatic pitch change was fitted, it would only move once, however from fine pitch to coarse on each flight. De Havilland let it be known that orders for this special racer would be welcomed.

Five Comets were ordered but only three left Mildenhall for Melbourne; G-ACSS, flown by Tom Campbell Black and Charles W. A. Scott won the race in 70hr 54min, proving conclusively that the Comet had a range of over 2,900 miles at a speed of 200mph.

Two airliners, a Boeing 247D flown by Roscoe Turner and Clyde Pangbourne, and a standard KLM Douglas DC-2 flown by Captains Parmentier and Moll, were entered. The DC-2 arrived at Melbourne, with three fare paying passengers, to finish second, 19hr 19min after the custom-built racing Comet.

When the aviation world had recovered from the shock of seeing a standard airliner matching the performance of an all-out racing machine, de Havillands began to analyse the situation.

Francis St Barbe, the sales director, observed, 'What an appalling thing to have

to do — design a little racer to compete with production passenger airliners!' The press commented caustically upon the state of the art in Britain pointing out that none of the front line machines in service with the national carrier had been sold to any other operator, being built in small numbers for Imperial Airways.

De Havilland wrote to the Air Ministry suggesting that they should build a high speed transport aircraft to compete on the air routes of the world, and inviting some form of financial assistance. No great enthusiasm for the proposal was forthcoming and not until January 1936 was an order placed for two of the airliners which the company had proposed, at a price which meant that DH would bear over half the development cost.

Deutsche Luft Hansa was fast developing the European routes with *Tante Ju* 'Aunty Ju', as the Ju52/3m was affectionately known. Many Germans had settled in South America and it was a matter of national pride that they should be able to return to the Fatherland by a German airline. The first stage was an air mail service, whilst the wealthier passengers could travel by the *Graf Zeppelin* until aircraft had the range to be practicable.

By the middle of the decade the huddle of huts used as a terminal at many aerodromes served by the international

67

67

The DH88 Comet racer, a superbly streamlined, low wing monoplane with two seats in tandem, was the first British aeroplane to combine a retractable undercarriage, flaps and a variable pitch propeller, rudimentary though the Ratier VP unit was. The blades were moved into fine pitch by a bicycle pump, after take-off as the machine gathered speed, increasing air pressure on a disc in the front of the spinner released air pressure so that a powerful spring could move the blades into coarse pitch. A balked landing was hazardous as the pilot could not change to fine pitch in the air.

The wing was a structural tour-de-force in its day, it served as a model for the Albatross in 1937 and the legendary Mosquito three years later.

Planked on both upper and lower surfaces to produce a very thin stiff structure, spars as such, were vestigial and were in the form of spacer webs. The fuselage was a wooden monocoque with flat sides and a curved upper decking.

G-ACSS the winner of the MacRobertson Race, is being rebuilt, at the time of writing, to flying condition. With two 230hp Gipsy Six R engines, the Comet had a maximum speed of 237mph, cruised at 220mph with a range of 2,975 miles.

The photograph shows Amy and Jim Mollison's DH 88 Comet at Mildenhall prior to the England to Australia Air Race in 1934.
Richard T. Riding

IMPERIAL AIRWAYS

THROUGH AFRICA
IN DAYS INSTEAD OF WEEKS

the railway terminal was usually an impressive building so the air traveller must be equally impressed.

Hard standings in front of the terminal were the focus of activity as the air liners taxied to embark and disembark their passengers. At Croydon a covered boarding way was wheeled to the entrance door to protect them from slipstream blast if the engines were running, and due ceremony was observed when a 'Hannibal' class aircraft departed. A smartly dressed official marched forward to salute the captain, signifying that the machine was fit to taxi out as soon as the green light appeared at the control tower. The small Civil Air Ensign flying from a staff above the flightdeck was lowered as the venerable transport moved off.

The airlines published passenger lists which often included famous names — Croydon to Paris was the glamour route, of interest to the gossip columnists who concentrated upon minor royalty, film and stage stars; mercifully, the TV personality had not appeared, Eastern potentates, business and military men appeared in the glossy magazines, occasionally, to the embarrassment of some enjoying illicit frolics on the Continent. It was good for trade and probably encouraged the timid to fly.

The captain, very smart in gold braid,

carriers had been replaced by modern purpose-built edifices which reflected civic, indeed, international, pride in the role of the city in the new era of travel. After all,

68

An Imperial Airways poster.
British Airways

was a god-like figure, even if his pay was derisory, as was often the case. It was paradoxical that, although the passengers were generally wealthy people, they were flattered by being able to converse with the pilot as he visited the cabin after take-off — the airborne equivalent, presumably, of the 'captain's table syndrome' of the ocean liners.

Capt J. H. Orrell, formerly chief test pilot of A. V. Roe, was an Imperial Airways pilot in the 1930s, he told the author that on long distance routes passengers stayed overnight in good hotels. Jimmy Orrell said, 'We were very decent to our customers, the Captain was expected to take a keen personal interest in the welfare of his passengers and always had a dinner jacket in his luggage.

'Navigational aids were rudimentary or non-existent, so we made all the decisions based upon the principle that the mail may be lost but not mislaid, the passengers may be delayed but not lost!'

Looking through the Imperial Airways posters of the period one is struck by the high quality of the designs, produced by eminent artists such as Barnett Freedman and P. G. Lawler, and the major emphasis placed upon the Paris route.

Engines were becoming more reliable, a very important factor, as the days when a forced landing could be made safely in a convenient field were passing, so weather forecasting and reporting en route became necessary. The ability to fly in bad weather, and at night, in safety was crucial to the establishment of air travel as a reliable transport system.

The end of the first half of this exciting decade saw the airlines in a fairly healthy state, developing fast throughout the world. America had scored a major success with the Douglas DC-2, destined to become one of the world's greatest transport aeroplanes. Trans-Pacific routes were also being developed by Pan Am using the Sikorsky S40 and S42 flying boats, soon to be joined by the superb Martin M130 powered by four Pratt and Whitney Twin Wasp radial engines of 830hp each. It had a wing span of 130ft, a range of 3,200 miles and cruised at 163mph with a crew of five. Between 14 and 41 passengers could be carried, according to the stage length. This handsome aircraft was of all metal construction and was stabilised on the water by sponsons rather than vulnerable wing tip floats.

Germany was developing the Junkers Ju86 all metal transport and it was abundantly clear that the United States and Germany would be the trend setters for years to come.

69
The first aircraft to span the Pacific in regular commercial operations in 1936, the Martin M130 'China Clipper', carried 41 passengers over a range of 3,200 miles. It cruised at 157mph and was powered by four 950hp Pratt and Whitney Wasp engines. A year after the three Pan Am Clippers entered service they had carried 1,986 passengers and 500,000lb of freight over 2¾ million miles.
PanAmerican World Airways

Continued Expansion

A change in the policy of the British Government had led, in 1936, to British Airways flying European routes hitherto the monopoly of Imperial Airways. Railway Air Services concentrated upon UK internal services with its fleet of de Havilland Dragons, Dragon Rapides and Express Air Liners. In a sense, this operator had the most difficult of tasks, with a large number of landings and take-offs over a limited mileage, often flown in bad weather with industrial haze at their destinations. The absence of good landing aids was a serious handicap, nevertheless the line had an enterprising and competent group of crews who were proud of their ability to fly in dirty weather.

Typical of the techniques they developed was one for landing at Ronaldsway, on the coast of the Isle of Man. With the trailing radio aerial reeled out the pilot would fly towards the aerodrome, directed by the operator in the tower who was taking a bearing on the transmissions. The altimeter was carefully set to the height of Ronaldsway above sea level. As soon as the ground operator reported the aircraft overhead, the pilot would turn and fly out to sea and descend slowly along a course agreed with the tower.

The aircraft radio operator would lightly grip the aerial cable, and, as he felt the lead weight hit the sea, it would be clear that the aeroplane was 100ft above the water. The pilot would then continue his descent for another 75ft. If, at 25ft, he could see the waves, he would turn back towards the aerodrome and, with the man in the tower guiding him by the radio bearings, he would continue his approach until the threshold was in sight and the landing made safely. Unfortunately, there were few aerodromes where this technique could be adopted.

Various attempts had been made over the years to solve the problem of blind landing — devices ranged from weights suspended from aircraft to give warning on an indicator that ground contact was imminent. In 1921, Professor Lindemann,

later Lord Cherwell, recommended a line of barrage balloons, at descending heights, to offer a visual glide path. In 1925, Capt Gordon Olley, flying a Handley Page W8 from Paris, safely landed at Croydon in thick fog, guided by signal flares fired from the terminal. This could not, of course, be considered as a technique for normal operations.

The major problem which delayed the introduction of fog and bad weather

70

70
The radio operator's station on *Canopus. Short Bros Ltd*

71
Short S23 Empire flying boat. The prototype, G-ADHL *Canopus*, was first flown by John Lankester Parker on 3 July 1936. Powered by four Bristol Pegasus 920hp engines these advanced aircraft were very successful and popular with passengers. Luxuriously appointed with a low noise level in the cabins, an exceptional cuisine was served upon fine china, and linen table cloths. A posting as a steward to an Empire boat was a prized promotion and demanded the highest standard. Any sloppiness, even a cough in the wrong place, meant demotion to tourist class. En route, over night stops were made and passengers accommodated in floating hotels. Up to 24 passengers were carried at a cruising speed of 165mph. The range was 1,500 miles. *Short Bros Ltd*

71

72
The Short Mayo composite aircraft. Flight tests of *Maia*, the lower component, and *Mercury*, the seaplane, took place in January 1938 and the first separation was successfully achieved on 6 February 1938. In July, *Mercury*, under the command of Capt D. C. T. Bennett (later to become commanding officer of the RAF wartime Pathfinder Force) flew 2,930 miles from Foynes to Boucherville, Canada in 20hr 20min. *British Airways*

73
Germany pioneered the use of depot ships to compensate for the inadequate range of the transatlantic marine aircraft. On 3 February 1934 a twin diesel-engined Dornier Wal flying boat first flew to South America, landing astern of the depot ship *Westfalen*, it was hoisted aboard by crane, refuelled and launched from a catapult over the bow. By 25 August 1935 four million letters had been carried across the South Atlantic in the course of 100 flights.

Later the large Blohm and Voss Ha139 was operated in the same way. The photograph, taken from the ship, shows the lifting shackle about to be attached. *Lufthansa*

landing aids was the lack of a really accurate approach guidance device. This had to await the arrival of electronics into the technical armoury. In America, however, in 1935, work began on the US Signal Corps System SCS51. This was developed into the very effective Instrument Landing system, ILS, which came to Britain with the US Air Force in World War 2. It consists of a pair of radio guidance beams — one, the localiser, which tells the pilot the direction in which to steer; the other, the glideslope, directs his descent at an angle of, usually, 3°, whilst two radio markers indicate his position on the approach.

The entry of British Airways to the European routes emphasised again the obsolescence of the Imperial Airways fleet. A curious clause in the BA contract called upon the line to operate aircraft capable of 200mph, so, as British builders were too busy with rearmament contracts to consider such an aeroplane, the new machines had to be bought abroad. The Lockheed 10A Electra was ordered for the London-Paris route. This 10-passenger, all-metal low wing monoplane had built a fine reputation in the USA as Lockheed's answer to the Boeing 247, and its price was lower than any other machine in its class. Its success was immediate. The first operator was North-West Airlines, in 1934; altogether 149 were built and they served throughout the world.

With a cruising speed of 190mph, the Electra reduced Imperial Airways flight time to Paris from 2hr 20min to 1hr 30min and was the first British-registered aircraft to offer first and second class accommodation.

Britain's first venture into building modern all-metal civil aircraft was the outcome of Imperial Airways decision to take full advantage of the 1934 Empire Air Mail Scheme. From 1937, all mail for the Empire would be carried by Imperial Airways without any surcharge, the cost being borne by the government. The sheer volume of projected traffic would require many more aircraft with greatly increased speed, range and payload. Realising that the state of the airfields en route would seriously inhibit a regular landplane service, an order was placed with Short

Brothers of Rochester, for 28 S23 Empire flying boats with four Bristol Pegasus radial engines. In an unprecedented show of confidence they were ordered straight off the drawing board, reducing considerably the delivery time for the boats which were to cost £50,000 each.

In all, 31 'C' class boats were built, Qantas buying six of them. The first scheduled service took place on 30 October 1936 when *Canopus* flew from Alexandria to Brindisi. The short interval of five months between first flight and entry into service speaks volumes for the ability of the designers of these magnificent flying boats. Arthur Gouge, later Sir Arthur, was the chief designer.

There can be no doubt that travel by flying boat was an experience vastly more enjoyable than travel by landplane — if the seas were not too rough! The sensation of take-off with the boat roaring across the water with clouds of spray flying past the windows was very exhilarating. Suddenly, the spray level would drop as she rose on the step and both wingtip floats came clear of the water. Acceleration was quite marked at this stage as she skimmed along on the planing bottom to lift smoothly into the air.

It was an experience to be relished, but, sadly, one in the past. On the debit side, flying at low altitude meant that the aircraft was susceptible to turbulence, which, in tropical areas, could be very unpleasant. All 28 'Empire' class flying boats of Imperial Airways were in service by the end of 1937, the year which followed the first trans-Pacific passenger flights by the Pan American Martin M130 flying boats.

To overcome the problem of inadequate range for the trans-Atlantic service, Maj R. H. Mayo, Imperial Airways General Technical Manager, suggested a composite aircraft. A modified Empire flying boat would carry a smaller long range seaplane on its back to launch it in flight, the combined power of the eight engines being used to lift the heavily loaded seaplane off the water.

The trials were successful but as the scheme was quite uneconomic, it was soon abandoned in favour of Sir Alan Cobham's much more realistic flight refuelling scheme which he had pioneered with his Airspeed Courier in 1933. Cobham refined the technique in the following years and

trans-Atlantic flights were carried out with the 'Empire' boats, *Cabot* and *Caribou*, which took aboard 800gal of fuel from a Handley Page Harrow tanker after take-off from Foynes.

Airships were still strong contenders for the role of trans-oceanic luxury carriers in Germany. By the end of 1936 the *Graf Zeppelin* had flown over 620,000 miles in 578 flights totalling 16,000 flying hours and had never injured a passenger.

This airship was not large enough for the trans-Atlantic crossing on a regular basis so the Zeppelin Company built the LZ129 *Hindenburg* for the New York route. It was hoped that the Americans would supply non-flammable helium gas to inflate this giant ship, but they refused to do so. During 1936 she flew 10 scheduled flights to New York and seven to Rio de Janeiro and, in May 1937 she left Frankfurt with 36 passengers, for Lakehurst, New Jersey.

In the early evening she slowly and majestically approached the American airfield, with a ground crew of over 200 men ready to catch her lines and ease her to the mooring mast. The passengers crowded at the windows to catch a glimpse of friends awaiting their arrival. Capt Preuss valved off hydrogen and dropped ballast to adjust the trim and the lines were dropped from the airship. Suddenly, the onlookers were horrified to see a huge flame emerge from the hull, near the tail, which dropped to the ground as the fireball spread right forward, with the ship almost vertical; it was destroyed in seconds. Miraculously 62

74
Short S23 *Cabot* being refuelled by a Handley Page Harrow tanker. *Flight Refuelling Ltd*

74

75
The Focke-Wulf Fw200 Condor.
In August 1938, this aircraft,
with most of the passenger
accommodation filled with long
range petrol tanks, flew
3,690 miles, from Berlin to New
York, in 24hr 36min, averaging
150mph. The flight was made
against fairly strong headwinds
and was the first non-stop flight
across the Atlantic by a
commercial aeroplane. The
return flight was made in
19hr 55min, averaging 185mph.
Lufthansa

76
A Bloch 220 at Croydon in 1938.
In the background can be seen a
DH90 Dragonfly. With a distinct
resemblance to the Douglas
DC-1 which had flown two
years earlier, the 220 used
components of the Bloch 210
bomber. It was powered with
two Gnome Rhône radial
engines of 985hp each and
carried 16 passengers at a
cruising speed of 174mph. The
range was 870 miles. Re-
engined with 1,200hp Wright
Cyclones and renumbered 221,
some served on Air France's
European routes just after the
war.
*London Borough of Sutton
Library*

of the 97 persons on board managed to
escape from the wreck of the luxurious
vessel.

This disaster marked the end of an era.
No more rigid airships were built as it had
become quite clear that the heavier than air
machine could be developed for long
distance flying with none of the
disadvantages of the ungainly dirigible.

The most advanced German airliner of
the time was the Focke-Wulf Fw200
Condor. The United States, Germany and
France were all working towards the
four-engine low wing monoplane formula
of all-metal airliner, and aeronautical
technology had reached a stage, by the
mid-1930s, when a design could be
produced with reasonable certainty that
the new aeroplane would be capable of
achieving the objectives with the minimum
amount of modification — there were a
number of exceptions to this optimistic
theory but the Fw200 was certainly not one
of them. Kurt Tank, the talented technical
director of Focke-Wulf, who was also a

skilled pilot (he carried out the test flights
of his outstanding World War 2 Fw190
fighter) decided to use a high aspect ratio
wing for maximum efficiency and, initially,
four Pratt and Whitney radial engines.

Tank himself made the first flight on
22 July 1937 and the test programme
progressed very smoothly — a considerable
achievement as the company had only built
small aircraft hitherto. A batch of Fw200s
was built with BMW radial engines of
720hp each, to give a cruising speed of 185
to 230mph, according to the stage length,
with 26 passengers.

DDL, the Danish airline, and Lufthansa
began operations with the Condor in the
summer of 1938 and the trans-Atlantic
flight of the Condor D-ACON created
worldwide interest. A *New York Times*
editorial predicted that one day the news of
such flights would not appear in headlines,
but alongside the shipping notices on the
inside pages. It would have seemed
inconceivable at that time, to imagine that
within 50 years the shipping notices would
almost disappear and the trans-Atlantic
flights become so commonplace that no
mention of them appeared anywhere other
than in the airline timetable.

When the war broke out Condor
production was switched to the military
versions for transport and commerce
raiding duties over the Atlantic. Over 280
civil and military Fw200s were built.

Another outstanding German transport
of this period was the Junkers Ju90. The
prototype of this 40-seat diesel-powered
aircraft, developed from the Ju89 four-
engined bomber, first flew in August 1937
but crashed in 1938. Later versions with
BMW radial engines went into service with

Deutsche Luft Hansa on the Berlin-Vienna route and were occasionally seen at Croydon.

Germany was unique in its work on diesel engines for aircraft. Before World War 1 Junkers was building experimental units. In 1931 the first practical compression ignition engine was installed in a Junkers F24 single-engined freighter and, by 1934, there were 14 such installations in service.

Lufthansa was the only airline to operate diesel-engined aircraft. As petrol engines became more reliable and efficient, with an increasingly favourable power/weight ratio, the diesel engine disappeared from civil aviation.

On 21 May 1938 the elegant Dornier Do26 four-engined, all-metal flying boat was flown for the first time. An interesting feature of this machine was the shallow hull, superbly streamlined, which necessitated the rear Junkers Jumo diesel engines being tilted upwards for take-off to protect the propellers from heavy spray. The Do26 proved to have adequate range for trans-Atlantic routes but, as with so many promising designs of this period, the outbreak of war in 1939 terminated further work upon it.

France tended to lag behind mainstream development in the late 1930s. In 1936 the three-engined Dewoitine 338 low wing all-metal monoplane was introduced. This was derived from an earlier Dewoitine trimotor, the D333, of which three were built with fixed undercarriages in 1934. The D338 was an attractive aeroplane powered by Wright Cyclones, built under licence by Hispano-Suiza, each developing 650hp. It had a retractable undercarriage

and seated up to 22 passengers with a crew of three or four. On Air France's African services 15 passengers were carried and on Far Eastern routes there was accommodation for 12 people, six of them in sleeper type seats. In total 31 were built and Air France operated eight of them as late as 1946 whilst awaiting re-equipment with more modern aircraft.

In 1935 two fine French machines made their first flights: the Bloch 220 twin-engined airliner and its smaller compatriot, the Caudron C445 Goëland which was one of the most successful European commercial aircraft of the decade. Although only 16 Bloch 220s were built they were widely used on Air France's European services, often being seen at Croydon.

Savoia Marchetti's first four-engined airliner was the S74 of which only three were built for use by Ala Littoria. The 30-seat SM75 followed in 1937. This reverted to the trimotor formula so characteristic of this constructor. It retained the slightly hump-backed appearance of its predecessors and the rounded fin and straight edged rudder which was probably the least attractive element in the design of the Savoia aircraft. It was a very fast machine; one of them — I-TALO — initiating the modern cult of 'personalised' registration letters — set up a world speed record in 1939 by flying a 22,000lb load a distance of 1,250 miles at an average speed of 205.6mph.

Later, this machine, which had three 1,000hp Alfa Romeo radial engines, set a world record for distance on a closed circuit, 8,083 miles being flown in 57hr 35min. The aeroplane was, of course, a

77
Dornier Do26 flying boat. With four 600hp Jumo diesel engines this graceful mail carrier cruised at 193mph and had the remarkable range of 5,590 miles with a crew of five and a payload of 1,985lb, only 4.5% of its all-up weight.

Note the retractable floats and the aft engines canted upward to reduce spray impact on the propellers when taking off and landing. *Lufthansa*

flying petrol tank but it showed the way
ahead.

The development of commercial aviation
in Russia was stimulated by the vast size of
the country with virtually no land
communications. Aeroflot was formed in
1923, as the successor to Dobrolet; by 1935
110,000 passengers and 11,000 tons of
freight had been carried. Aircraft design
was a fairly primitive art and the mainstay
of the line was the ANT-9 trimotor which
was widely used in the Soviet Union from
1929 and was based upon European
designs.

A remarkable development in 1932 was a
propaganda exercise to commemorate the
anniversary of the writer Maxim Gorky's
first literary success, Andrei Tupolev's
bureau designed the ANT-20, named
Maxim Gorky. This 206ft span colossus
weighed 41.3 tons and was powered by
eight engines totalling 7,200hp. With its
printing plant, photographic studio, radio
transmitting station, cinema and facilities
for neon displays under the wings the
machine operated for a year before being
destroyed in a mid-air collision in 1935.
Three more were built, but these had only
six engines.

Influenced by the Boeing 247, Tupolev
flew, in 1935, his first all-metal transport,
the ANT-35. One was shown at the Paris Air
Show in the following year, but visitors,
accustomed to the high standards of finish
of American and European aircraft, were
highly critical of it, although its general
form was very modern. With two 850hp
radial engines it cruised at 210mph with 10
passengers.

In the USA competition was intense
among the airlines and the constructors.
American Airlines, realising that its Curtiss
Condor sleeper services were hopelessly
out-dated by the new DC-2, asked Douglas
to consider a sleeper version of the new
airliner.

On 17 December 1935 the Douglas
Sleeper Transport was flown for the first
time. Basically it was a DC-2 with a
fuselage lengthened by 30.25in and
widened by 26in to accommodate 14
berths. The wing was increased in span
and strengthened and a larger tail unit was
designed. A version of it for daytime use
was known as the DC-3. Thus the immortal
'Gooney Bird' appeared on the aviation
scene which was never quite the same
again. It dominated the air routes and, for
years, had hardly any competition.
Between 1935 and 1937, when production
ceased, 10,654 had been built by Douglas,
485 in Japan under licence whilst 2,000 of
them had been built by Lisunov in Russia
as the Li-2.

By the time the United States entered the
war in December 1941, 260 aircraft out of a
total US airline fleet strength of 322 —
80.7% — were DC-3s. In 1939, 90% of the
world's airline passengers were carried in
this remarkable aeroplane. One might ask
why it was such a unique machine — a very
difficult question to answer. Donald
Douglas was undoubtedly a very able
engineer and a designer who 'could see the
spray, as C. G. Grey put it in the context of
Hessell Tiltman's Airspeed Courier.

Tiltman visited the Douglas plant in 1934
and later, discussed his visit with Anthony

80

Fokker, who was also interested in the possibility of building the DC-2 under licence. Tiltman told the author that in spite of his own preoccupation with 'cleaning up' his own aeroplanes, Fokker's close inspection of the DC-2 had left him with a sense of shame about his own poor efforts in comparison. He had taken the trouble to clean up the general outline of his aircraft and to cut off obvious outgrowths which threw out spray, but in the DC-2, the designers had studied every detail. They had won half a mile an hour here by cleaning up one thing, another mile or two by smoothing off something else, and had gone over the whole design in incredible detail. Douglas told Tiltman that the original door handle had been a streamlined bullet projecting into the slipstream, he was doubtful about this shape and also about the use of round head rivets, for economic reasons, on the outer skin. So he spread glutinous engine oil over those parts of the aeroplane where he suspected that turbulence was developing; after flight test the path of the oil streaks showed him where improvements had to be made. The door handle was recessed, and, in certain areas, countersunk rivets were used. The structural engineering was also extremely good with almost unlimited fatigue life and fairly easy maintenance procedures, the passengers, pilots and groundcrews were happy with the aeroplane and the price was right. All simple formulae for success but not easily emulated, as the continuing quest for a DC-3 Dakota replacement proves.

Douglas's leadership in the airline

79
DC-3 Flagship Sleeper. Powered with 900hp Wright Cyclone engines, or with the equivalent Pratt and Whitney Wasps, the DC-3 had almost the same performance as the smaller DC-2. Donald Douglas's policy of aerodynamic refinement and increase in size resulted in a machine which could carry a payload 50% larger than that of its predecessor for an increase of only 10% in operating costs. *American Airlines*

80
The interior of the Douglas DC-3 Sleeper Transport. Berths for 14 passengers were provided. In its daytime configuration the type could carry from 20 to 28 passengers and was the 'jumbo' of its day. *McDonnell Douglas*

81
The DC-4 prototype in flight. *McDonnell Douglas*

81

comfort by avoiding low level turbulence.
The prototype met a disastrous end in
March 1939 when it suffered an explosive
decompression of the pressure cabin and
crashed killing all on board, including the
technical director and chief engineer of
KLM who were at the Boeing plant to
evaluate the aircraft for service on their
long-distance routes. Nevertheless, this
superbly streamlined airliner entered
service with TWA in mid-1940.
Only 10 were built and it
proved a good work-horse
remaining in service
until the 1960s.

82
A de Havilland DH90 Dragonfly
operated by Rhodesian and
Nyasaland Airways. *BAe*

83
De Havilland DH91 Albatross in
flight. *Aeroplane Monthly*

market stung Lockheed into retaliation
with the Super Electra, the Lockheed 14,
which was probably more famous as the
wartime Hudson reconnaissance bomber.
Clarence L. Johnson, Lockheed's chief
designer, realised that, to achieve major
success in a field dominated
by Douglas, a very
advanced aeroplane
would be required.
He had the
advantage that the
Lockheed 10 Electra had
already achieved considerable
success with the airlines who
leaned towards 'brand loyalty'. Speed was
important, so wing loading tended to be
rather high. Johnson decided to use Fowler
flaps. These effective high-lift devices slid
out from the trailing edges of the wing on
curved guides, increasing substantially the
lifting area and altering the section of the
wing to give greater lift.

Many domestic airlines in the USA
operated the Lockheed 14 and it found a
good market in Europe, KLM being first in
the field, closely followed by British
Airways, Sabena, LOT in Poland, and the
Irish line, Aer Lingus Teoranta.

The eclipse of the Boeing 247 by the
Douglas DC-2 and DC-3 had been a severe
blow to Bill Boeing. He decided to design a
machine to a bomber specification which
could form the basis of a large four-
engined airliner. The Boeing 299, the
forerunner of the famous Flying Fortress
bomber, was the first to be flown, followed
in December 1938 by the Model 307 civil
aircraft. Pan Am and TWA were interested.
38 passengers were accommodated in the
first pressurised cabins, designed to 'cruise
above the weather', to improve passenger

Douglas continued to shine in the transport aircraft firmament. Encouraged, originally, by Pan Am, TWA, Eastern Airlines and American Airlines, who each agreed to pay $100,000 towards the development costs of a new four-engined airliner, Douglas produced the DC-4E. With a wingspan of 138ft 3in this large aeroplane was powered by four 1,450hp Pratt and Whitney twin-row Hornet radial engines but carried only 52 passengers by day and 30 by night.

Structurally, it was interesting. It was becoming obvious that one of the serious potential problems facing large aeroplanes

84

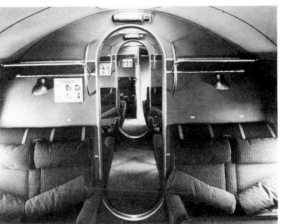

was the likelihood of fatigue failure, particularly in the wing spars, where the continual flexing of the wing weakens the metal, causing cracks and ultimate failure. The Douglas wing was of multi-spar construction so that, in the event of a crack developing in one section of the wing, there were sufficient load bearing members to avoid catastrophic failure. The fuselage was an all-metal monocoque with provision for pressurisation in production machines. Accommodation was palatial with a stateroom and well appointed washrooms. Under the floor were freight and baggage holds. Trailing edge flaps extended almost from tip to tip of the wing and triple fins and rudders on a dihedralled tailplane ensured directional control in the 'engine out' condition.

The outstanding feature of the DC-4E was the tricycle undercarriage which set the pattern for almost all future multi-engined aeroplanes.

In May 1939 United Airlines took it over for evaluation on their routes. It proved to be a disappointment, in spite of its

84
Frobisher, the flagship of the Imperial Airways fleet, at Croydon. The photograph shows clearly the superb lines of the type and the clean engine installation. It was the first aircraft to bear the single Speedbird emblem which appeared on all aircraft of Imperial Airways, BOAC and British Airways long-haul services until it was rejected by the American design consultants, Landor Associates, in 1984.

The HP42 in the background provides an interesting contrast in 'state of the art', having first flown only seven years before the de Havilland machine. *Aeroplane Monthly*

85
Cabin interior of *Frobisher*. *British Airways*

advanced specification. Maintenance was very difficult and costly, and, for such a large aircraft, its revenue earning capacity was quite inadequate. The airlines decided that a smaller machine was needed, so, from the basics of the DC-4E, the quite outstanding DC-4 emerged, too late to fly on the peacetime routes, but in time to make a valuable contribution to the logistics of deploying the American forces all over the world — and, to become the mainstay of long-haul airline operations immediately after the war.

The fuselage was much slimmer than the DC-4E and was of parallel form for most of its length. It set the pattern for mass production of transport aircraft in building a simple stressed skin 'tube' which could easily be varied in length according to the needs of the customer. Its directional stability, with the slim fuselage, was so good that the triple tail was unnecessary. Like the DC-4E it had powered controls, a development necessitated by the sheer size of aeroplanes and the excessive forces needed to move the control surfaces manually at the speeds which were being achieved.

Back in Britain, Imperial Airways was basking in the glow of success achieved with the 'Empire' flying boats, although their safety record on the routes was not one to be proud of — no blame, however, could be attached to the aircraft. Nevertheless they remained popular with their passengers and larger versions were being planned.

At the smaller end of the aeronautical spectrum, various manufacturers thought that a market existed for an aircraft which, today, we would call an executive transport. To a degree the Airspeed Courier met this description but was slightly too large.

The de Havilland Engine Company was busy developing its classic range of four and six cylinder in-line engines and, with worldwide servicing facilities available, these were the ideal engines for such aircraft. In August 1935 Heston Aircraft Co Ltd flew, for the first time, its Phoenix. This very handsome five-seat, strut-braced high-wing monoplane cruised at 125mph with a DH Gipsy Six engine developing 200hp. It was an expensive machine and only five were built.

The more successful de Havilland DH90 Dragonfly closely followed the Phoenix,

being flown for the first time on 12 August 1935. This very attractive biplane, with a strong family resemblance to the DH Dragon Rapide, followed the usual de Havilland principle of wooden construction, but the fuselage was a complete departure from previous designs, being a formed monocoque shell of plywood, with some internal stiffening of spruce members. The lower wing centre section was a strong cantilever carrying the engine and undercarriage mountings without the Rapide's diagonal bracing to the top of the fuselage.

The five occupants were carried in considerable luxury with enough room to change seats without difficulty, whilst the two 130hp Gipsy Major engines gave the machine a sparkling performance, a top speed of 144mph and the ability to maintain a ceiling of 2,100ft with a full load, on one engine.

The interesting feature of the Dragonfly from a structural point of view was the use of plywood moulded to a double curvature. Conventionally, it was accepted that plywood could be bent round a cylinder but not round a spherical form. It was found that if the laminated thin sheets were clamped between two appropriate dies before the adhesive had set, double curvature was feasible. Saunders Roe developed the technique commercially using synthetic resins cured under heat and pressure. Aft of the luggage compartment the shell, being of single curvature, was made of flat sheet, formed with stiffened radii at the corners to eliminate longerons. The stiffening was achieved by laminating, at the corners, tapered, overlapping strips of ply and bonding the lot together under pressure. Extreme stiffness was achieved and it was difficult to deform this very strong structure.

This beautiful aeroplane was quite expensive at £2,650 but it found a ready market among the wealthier private owners thoughout the world, with companies as an executive transport, and as an air taxi — an aspect of civil aviation which was developing. The Hon Mrs Victor Bruce's company, Air Dispatch Ltd, operated a fleet of six DH90s. One was owned by King Feisal of Iraq with the registration YI-HMK — the cult of personalised registrations was developing! Total production was 67, only 21 being

bought, initially, by British owners. Yet
again, de Havilland's world-wide product
support facilities stood the company in
good stead.

The Dragonfly's lineal successor was the
DH91 Albatross, thought by many to be the
most beautiful aeroplane ever built — for
sheer elegance it was unsurpassed until
Concorde appeared.

As was recorded earlier, de Havilland
had approached the Air Ministry after the
1934 MacRobertson Race with proposals
for a high speed airliner. Not until 1936
was a specification issued for two trans-
Atlantic mailplanes, with potential for
development into a fast airliner. The
contract required the transport of 1,000lb
of mail over a distance of 2,500 miles
against a continuous headwind of 40mph.
This exacting requirement necessitated a
high degree of aerodynamic efficiency as
the two main parameters were of crucial
importance and incompatible. High speed
had to be achieved with strict fuel economy
as speed could not be sacrificed in a long
range aeroplane carrying His Majesty's
Mails.

De Havilland's success in meeting the
specification with the DH91 was largely
due to its control over the design of the
airframe, the engines and the propellers —
by this time they were building American
Hamilton Standard controllable pitch
propellers under licence. That great artist
Arthur E. Hagg his team, and Charles
C. Walker, the talented chief engineer,
handled the overall design of the DH91
whilst Maj Frank Halford, the designer of
the Gipsy range of engines, was
responsible for the powerplant. He
proposed a new inverted Vee 12-cylinder

engine using the cylinder blocks of the very
successful Gipsy Six on a new crankcase. In
this way, the 525hp Gipsy King was
developed and thoroughly tested on rigs at
Stag Lane factory and at Hatfield. It was a
heavy engine but, with its unique reverse
flow cooling system which achieved one of
the cleanest engine installations ever seen
in an aeroplane, and the remarkable
aerodynamic refinement of the airframe,
gave the new aircraft a very high
performance.

Chief test pilot R. J. 'Bob' Waight flew the
prototype for the first time on 20 May 1937.
Handling was, in general, excellent,
although, on the climb the twin inset
rudders on a typical de Havilland tailplane
were not responsive. The tail unit was
altered to comprise two 'endplate' rudders
at the ends of a dihedralled, tapered
tailplane. This became standard, and
greatly improved the already beautiful
lines of the Albatross.

The superb streamlining was achieved
by a unique fuselage construction of a
plywood/balsa/plywood sandwich
moulded to double curvature. The 105ft
span, one-piece wing followed the
principles of the Comet wing in having a
thick upper and lower wooden planked skin
with minimal internal structure.

The retractable undercarriage was
undoubtedly the Achilles heel of this
interesting and advanced airliner. Each leg
was retracted inwards by means of an
electrically rotated screw jack attached to a
lever above the oleo leg hinge point. The
thin wing necessitated a very short lever so
side loads caused great strain upon the
operating mechanism.

Soon after the first flight of the Albatross,

86
The Armstrong Whitworth
AW27 Ensign. A single rudder
on such a large four engined
airliner, with the outer engines
well outboard, was, perhaps, a
surprising feature of this
handsome aeroplane.
Unfortunately the type was
seriously handicapped by
unreliable and underpowered
engines. *British Airways*

Bob Waight was killed in the diminutive TK4 racer, designed and built by the de Havilland Aeronautical Technical School. Geoffrey de Havilland Jnr was appointed to succeed him and took over the test programme of the new airliner. On one flight, he found that he could not lower the undercarriage mechanically or by the manual emergency system. He was forced to make a belly landing at Hatfield but fortunately little damage was done to the aircraft. Later, during overload tests, the fuselage broke through an exit door as Geoffrey was landing at Hatfield.

This was only a temporary embarrassment, the fuselage being returned to the mould and reassembled with additional stiffening members. The aeroplane flew again five weeks later.

The efficiency of the Albatross was outstanding. One yardstick was the number of gross ton miles per gallon of fuel used. The DH80 Puss Moth offered 18 to the gallon. The DH88 Comet lifted the figure to 25, but the Albatross achieved a remarkable 33. At a cruising speed of 210mph it flew 2½ miles on a gallon of fuel. Charles C. Walker had a penchant for describing complex aerodynamic phenomena in very simple terms, one of his classics was the proposition that if the exposed surface of the Albatross was represented by a sheet of glass of negligible thickness, it would only travel 49mph faster if it was drawn edgewise through the air by the 1,300 cruising horse power of the

engines — in other words the Albatross' top speed was 81% of what it would be if the aircraft was perfectly streamlined.

Two mail carriers and five airliners were built, the airliners forming the 'Frobisher' class in the service of Imperial Airways. They were the first aircraft to carry the Speedbird symbol which continued to grace Imperial Airways, BOAC and British Airways machines until its summary dismissal by the American design consultants called in to re-vamp the corporate image in 1984 — a move which many thought, with some justification, to be a heresy.

The airliners went into service on the Paris route in November 1938, later flying to Brussels and Zurich. The flight time to Paris was reduced to 53min at an average speed of 219mph. Brussels was reached in 48min and the Christmas mail was flown to Alexandria at an average speed of 219mph.

Passengers viewed the 'F' class with mixed feelings; by present day standards the seating was luxurious but cramped by comparison with the Handley Page 42s to which they were accustomed. The Pullman carriage atmosphere had gone, to be replaced by light coloured furnishings and comfortable modern armchairs with a cushion width of 20in. The cabin windows were 2ft 4½in wide. The flexing of the high aspect ratio wing caused a rather unpleasant motion in gusty air and de Havilland's hopes that the ply/balsa sandwich construction of the fuselage

87
Two Armstrong Siddeley products showing the size of the Ensign. *British Airways*

would reduce noise and vibration were not realised. In spite of these problems the Albatross was good for the prestige of Britain in the aviation world — it was a leap ahead in efficient airliner design.

On the outbreak of war the fleet was impressed, with all other civil aircraft, into National Air Communications and the machines were in service for months without hangar accommodation. De Havilland had stated that the plywood structure was hermetically sealed by a film of synthetic resin, claiming in the December 1938 issue of the *De Havilland Gazette*, which was entirely devoted to the new airliner (of which the company was, justifiably, very proud). 'A feature of the main aircraft structure is the almost complete absence of necessary maintenance attention to the wing and fuselage and the ease of repair to either. In any part of the world . . . standard repair schemes call for no special repair schemes of any kind. (sic)'

The last statement was probably true but the first one revealed a level of over-optimism quite unjustified by events. The company fell into the trap of fitting too few inspection panels into the structure and experienced the usual problem of water drainage holes in the wings and elsewhere becoming blocked. The general ineffectiveness of structural protection was not noticed until it was too late. Various crashes on war service reduced the fleet to four aircraft. *Frobisher*, the flagship, was destroyed by an arsonist at its Whitchurch base. The first signs of serious trouble emerged in 1941 when *Fiona* lost a section of the port wing root fairing due to the rotting of members to which it was fixed.

As late as 1942 the BOAC chief inspector was still satisfied that the main structural life of the wing and tail would be five years and, for the fuselage, 10 years. Time ran out for the 'F' class on 13 July 1943. *Fortuna*, with 15 on board, was on its final approach at Shannon, when Capt Moss lowered the undercarriage and selected full flap. Suddenly there was a loud report and the aircraft lost height, yawing to port. She crashed into a field alongside the River Fergus, sliding broadside until she stopped, miraculously with no serious injury to the occupants.

It was found that the structure was in poor condition, causing the flaps and their mountings to tear away. The surviving aircraft, *Fiona* and *Falcon*, were grounded and, later, broken up.

The chequered careers of these seven beauties were short, but they are recalled with deep admiration and respect by many who knew them. They left a priceless legacy of aerodynamic and structural experience which led to one of the outstanding aeroplanes of all time, the de Havilland DH98 Mosquito which was structurally very similar.

A project of much longer term than the Albatross had been initiated by Imperial Airways to meet the needs of the 1934 Empire Air Mail scheme. It was considered that the traffic growth could be met by a large, all-metal, four engined airliner, the Armstrong Whitworth AW27 Ensign. Powered by four 800hp Armstrong Siddeley Tiger radial engines, there were two versions — one with 40 seats for European routes, and the other, to be flown to the East with accommodation for 27 passengers by day or, alternatively, 20 on night flights. They were originally planned to fly in 1936, but interminable changes demanded by the airline, and various technical problems, delayed the first flight until January 1938 when Charles Turner Hughes and Eric Greenwood took the prototype into the air for the first time.

There were many difficulties at the test-flying stage, not the least of which was the realisation that the aircraft was under-powered; modifications delayed the Paris route proving trials until October 1938. A Christmas mail flight to Australia by three of the fleet proved an utter fiasco. *Egeria* required an engine change at Athens, *Elsinore* needed one at Karachi, and *Euterpe* only reached India.

The aeroplanes already delivered were returned to the builders. Not until the summer of 1939 were they seen on the routes again, this time with more powerful engines. Even these were inadequate for the important Middle East sectors. Some Ensigns were fitted with American Wright Cyclone engines but these proved to be a mistake as the particular mark of engine used was withdrawn from production early in the war, so spares were difficult to obtain.

Some of the fleet of 14 aircraft staggered on throughout the war, absorbing valuable man-hours in maintenance at vast expense. In 1947, the five survivors were scrapped at

The very handsome
de Havilland DH95 Flamingo in
wartime camouflage. *BAe*

Hamble where they had been assembled in
the shops of Air Service Training.

The Ensign was a very unlucky aeroplane
with good potential which could have been
exploited if Armstrong Whitworth had not
been so heavily committed to the
production of the Whitley bomber, if
suitable engines had been available and
had the war not intervened.

By the time the war was over, lightly
loaded big aeroplanes designed for grass
aerodromes were outdated by modern high
loaded transports designed for paved
runways which proliferated throughout the
world during the war.

The last metal aeroplane to go into
service in Britain before the war was the de
Havilland DH95 Flamingo twin engine high
wing monoplane designed by Arthur
Hagg's successor, R. E. Bishop. It cut right
across the American trend towards four
engines and low wings. First flown by
Geoffrey de Havilland Jnr on 28 December
1938, it was of orthodox stressed skin
construction designed to ensure that as
many parts as possible were
interchangeable; for example, the inner
stub wing could be fitted to either side — at
least that was the theory, not,
unfortunately borne out in practice when a
Flamingo had a mishap in Jersey!

Bristol Perseus sleeve valve engines were
fitted and it carried its 12-17 passengers in
considerable comfort at a top speed of
239mph, cruising at 184mph. An attractive
feature to operators and passengers was
the low ground clearance which made
embarkation very easy. Originally the
prototype had a central fin but flight trials
proved that directional stability with one
engine out was adequate without it.

Twenty Flamingos were laid down; one
was loaned to Guernsey and Jersey
Airways, and another was built for the
King's Flight. Some were converted to
communications machines for service with
the Royal Air Force and the Royal Navy.
One survived the war but was broken up in
1948. So, yet another promising design was
stultified by the war.

By September 1939, when World War 2
broke out, civil aviation had made immense
progress since its inception 20 years
previously, and only 36 years after the
Wright Brothers had launched their 'Flyer'
at Kitty Hawk, in North Carolina.

From the traditional forms of
construction of wire-braced wooden
frames covered by doped fabric, aeroplanes
had developed into complex, all-metal
machines seating up to 80 passengers in a
degree of comfort beyond imagination two
decades earlier, with the immediate
prospect of pressurised cabins designed to
reproduce at 20,000ft, conditions normally
experienced at 7,000ft.

The science of aerodynamics was
becoming less of a 'black art' as the
national research centres, such as the
British Royal Aircraft Establishment at
Farnborough, worked on basic
aerodynamic, thermodynamic and
structural problems, whilst the practical
application was carried out largely at such
places as the Aircraft and Armament
Experimental Establishment at
Martlesham Heath, Suffolk (it moved, on
outbreak of war, to Boscombe Down near

Salisbury) and at the Marine Aircraft Establishment at Felixstowe. Together with the invaluable work being carried out by the aircraft constructors in their own research departments knowledge was being extended with every new aeroplane which appeared.

Specialised research was in progress on radio communications, navigational equipment, blind flying aids and training aids such as the Link Trainer, whilst useful information was becoming available on the physiological effects of high altitude flying, and the effect of pressurised cabin environments, from the work in progress at the Physiological Laboratory of the Royal Air Force, soon to become the Institute of Aviation Medicine.

The voracious and desperate needs of war intensified the need for more and more data to solve ever increasing problems experienced in wartime operations. The solutions, in many cases, were directly applicable to civil aviation which could not have afforded to finance this work from its own profits.

The principal technical development was the acceptance of the stressed skin, cantilever monoplane configuration with supercharged engines driving controllable pitch propellers. A retractable undercarriage (the tricycle undercarriage had just arrived) with high lift devices to offset the effect of much higher wing loadings and reduce landing speeds was commonplace. These elements, along with the pressurised cabin, were the basis of future development until the arrival of the gas turbine which, by the end of 1938, was a practical reality. Frank Whittle had run his WU (Whittle Unit) at 16,500rpm for 30min and the Air Ministry Director of Scientific Research had been sufficiently impressed with it to recommend the production of an engine for flight trials.

Air travel had reached a stage among its fairly well-to-do customers where they were fairly blasé about it. Comfort was taken for granted and standards were high. Airliners were vehicles for travel, as was the ship, train or motor car, but not, so far, as safe or reliable as these older methods.

Safety and reliability depended upon several factors: aircrew competence, adequate air traffic control, high standards of maintenance of aircraft, engines and ancillary equipment. Adequate blind flying facilities were necessary, with efficient radio communication and aids for landing in bad weather. The Lorenz beam, first installed at Croydon in 1935, was a good starting point but it had limitations. Not until wartime experience with instrument landing system (ILS) had been distilled into a technique for airliners could it be said that night and bad weather landing had begun to emerge from the 'seat of the pants' era; effective though the techniques usually were, it was the exceptions that killed people and broke aeroplanes.

The new airliners, with their high wing loadings, required a longer run for take-off, and landed at a higher speed. As the undercarriages were retractable, the landing wheels had to be as small as possible, so green fields, which turned into quagmires in winter, were no longer adequate. Paved runways were built at airfields serving the major cities. Passenger handling facilities already existed in the form of architect-designed buildings to accommodate the airline offices as well as airport administration.

The companies recognised, at a very early stage, the value of a good and recognisable corporate image. Indeed, the airlines were well in advance of most commercial organisations, although the shipping lines and railways were also pioneers in 'image building'.

It is of interest to compare the high standards of graphic design commissioned by Imperial Airways with the contemporary standards of industrial design. Generally it was accepted that British industrial design was inferior to comparable continental work, particularly that being produced in countries influenced by the Bauhaus ideas of Professor Walter Gropius, although, as mentioned earlier, his principles of aesthetic design do not appear to have influenced the Junkers design team nearby at Dessau.

John Gloag, in his book *Industrial Art Explained* commented that most European countries were far ahead of England in the sections of industry that depend upon a working partnership with design. It may be true that this new industry, with none of the inhibitions of the Industrial Revolution, had itself been innovative — indeed, its survival and prosperity depended upon innovation — and had, consequently, transferred to its associated peripheral activities a similarly enterprising approach. In the second decade, Imperial Airways had been heavily criticised for its insufficiently enterprising publicity policy. To its credit the company took notice, and commissioned the leading British commercial artists to produce publicity material which was displayed throughout the world.

New aircraft were well promoted in posters and brochures, and what today would be called National Heritage subjects such as the Coronation, or a Royal event would be publicised abroad in several languages.

The International Air Transport Association and the International Civil Aviation Organisation were working towards standardised operating procedures throughout the world to ensure the maximum degree of safety and efficiency in the industry.

Aeroplanes were becoming increasingly expensive to buy and to run, so the cost of time spent on the ground had to be minimal. The short haul operators had a major vested interest in this aspect. To them, a quick turn-round was vital — a 40min period on the ground at the end of an international flight lasting many hours was not very significant, but on a stage length of 150 miles it would be intolerable.

The elements which determine speed of turn-round were (and, indeed, still are):

● Speed of disembarkation of passengers, luggage and freight.
● Time to clean cabin and empty toilets, whilst the galley is re-stocked with food.
● Time taken by engineers in checking aircraft for faults or rectifying faults reported by the crew.
● Time taken to re-fuel aircraft and re-embark passengers.

The most important and costly element in this schedule is the maintenance of the machine, both on the flight line and in the hangar where maintenance schedules are carried out to a strictly controlled programme laid down by the manufacturer and the Civil Airworthiness Authority.

The airframe and engine designers play a vital part in ensuring that equipment which requires regular inspection is easily accessible, preferably from the ground. Special tools may be necessary, and a part of the technical function is the preparation of comprehensive workshop and maintenance manuals all of which must be kept up to date. Any problems which arise, and are likely to recur, may require immediate modification action so a system must be set up which will inform operators immediately.

Aircraft manufacturers opened Service Schools where licensed Ground Engineers could obtain endorsements indicating their competence to maintain particular aeroplanes or engines.

The ease with which cabins can be cleaned is also partly dependent upon the design staff, but more so upon the techniques of the contractors who carry out the work.

Restocking the galley was a relatively straightforward operation and refuelling of the aircraft was expedited by the petrol companies who developed large capacity tankers capable of pumping fuel at high speed.

The number of aeroplanes outside the terminal, to receive and disembark their passengers, was increasing rapidly and becoming a source of congestion and delay. At Gatwick a terminal building was opened in 1936 to overcome the difficulty. Known as the Beehive, it was circular in plan; airliners taxied up to one of six designated positions around it, the passengers walking through radial covered ways to the aircraft. It was certainly the first such terminal in the UK, and probably in Europe. Postwar expansion at Gatwick left it outdated but it can still be seen near the main road which passes the new terminal.

In 1939 the city of Birmingham opened its new terminal at Elmdon, south of the city. The building was based upon the style of Tempelhof, Berlin, and had two cantilever canopies under which aircraft could taxi so that passengers were protected from the weather. This, too, proved inadequate when traffic at Elmdon increased after the war.

Cargo carrying operations were developing rapidly in the years before the war, so terminal design had to take this service into consideration at an early stage in planning.

But at 11.00am on Sunday 3 September 1939 Prime Minister Neville Chamberlain broadcast to the British nation the grave news that a state of war existed with Germany. The navigation lights and beacons were extinguished throughout Europe and civil aviation came to a standstill.

World War 2 and its Aftermath

An organisation which has considerable influence upon the shape of civil aviation, both commercially and technically, is the International Air Transport Association. Formed in 1919 by the managements of leading airlines, its objective was the promotion of civil aviation as a viable and efficient means of transport with a co-ordinated international approach to all its problems.

It soon brought to its councils the relationship between airlines and third parties, such as governments, the public, insurance interests and other forms of transport. In 1931 IATA began to study standardisation of airfield facilities in the context of flight safety and economical operating costs.

The technical committees passed to manufacturers, governments and other interested bodies detailed specifications of aircraft materials, instrumentation and cockpit layouts, technical symbols and fuels. An important event was the issue of drawings for a standard fuel tank filler cap, and an even more fundamental decision that throttle controls should always be moved forwards to increase power and rearwards to reduce it. There had been a number of serious accidents due to confusion in the cockpit.

Blind landing was high on the technical agenda. In 1935 IATA recommended that the standard landing aid should comprise ultra short wave radio beacons, adaptable for both audible and visual presentation on the flightdeck. These, and other proposals, formed the basis of representations made by the airlines to their respective governments. In an international business, standardisation was essential if all the participants were to enjoy the maximum benefit from their investment.

The outbreak of World War 2 marked the end of the first, and venturesome, phase of airliner development and it became a forcing ground for new technology in the desperate contest for air superiority. Developments which would have taken many peacetime years to accomplish came

to fruition in a relatively short time, and were perfected under demanding active service conditions.

The Atlantic Ocean was a major barrier, presenting a challenge to those who could not accept that the stately but slow ocean liners must be the conventional way to travel between Europe and America. Flying boats had demonstrated their potential in a limited way, but no landplane had shown any ability to fly the Atlantic with a load of fare-paying passengers and adequate fuel reserves for diversion. Flight refuelling was an interesting possibility but navigation was difficult, and the weather over the ocean was a serious problem which defied the forecasters. Particularly risky was the East to West flight against the prevailing winds.

From the beginning of the war America supplied Britain with aeroplanes and other military equipment under the Lease-Lend agreement. The smaller aircraft were loaded on freighters which suffered appalling losses from German U boats and Focke-Wulf Condor commerce raiders. It became essential to fly twin-engined machines across, using staging posts in Canada and Greenland, en route to Prestwick on the west coast of Scotland.

Thus the Atlantic Ferry Organisation, ATFERO, was formed and in November 1940 the first Hudsons, the military version of the Lockheed 14, were flown across by BOAC pilots. Later, RAF crews took over whilst BOAC operated the Return Ferry service with Liberator bombers fitted with

89
An Avro York of Hunting-Clan Air Transport Ltd about to commence its take-off run. The attractive livery included the Clan shipping line logo forward and the British Civil Aviation ensign on the fins. The two streamlined fairings above the cabin contain the loop aerials for the direction finding radio installation. BOAC operated a fleet of Yorks, 13 of which were 12-berth sleepers for the London-Johannesburg 'Springbok' route. In the freight role they served until the end of 1957. 90,000 passengers were carried in 44 million miles of route flying. The high density seating version could carry up to 65 passengers. Cruising speed was 251mph and the range 2,700 miles.
257 were built. *BAe*

89

90,91
Many early postwar European airliners were developed from prewar or wartime designs. Lufthansa, for example, which was not permitted to fly until April 1955, started its operations with Convair 340s for short-haul routes and Lockheed Super Constellations on the long-haul services. A few DC-3s were used (90) — note the German flag on the fin and the absence of the stork logo.

Alitalia also used DC-3s and the earlier SM95C. Here (91) the Fiat G212 is illustrated. One of the last large trimotor propeller-driven aircraft to be built, the G212 had 1,065hp Pratt & Whitney Twin Wasp engines and carried up to 34 passengers at a cruising speed of 186mph. Range was 1,864 miles. Like the SM95C, only 12 were built for civil use.
Lufthansa; Alitalia.

92
Air Cdre Sir Frank Whittle KBE, CB, MA, FRS, Hon MiMechE, Hon FRAeS, Hon DSc (Cantab), Hon DSc (Oxon, Manchester, Leicester), Hon LLD (Edin), Hon DTech (Trondheim), RAF (Retd), receiving the Churchill Gold Medal at the Royal Automobile Club in October 1952.
PA Reuters via Richard T. Riding

93
The de Havilland design team studying a model of the Mosquito. From left to right: C. C. Walker CBE, AMICE, Hon FRAeS, Director and Chief Engineer, joined Geoffrey de Havilland in 1915, retiring in 1955; Capt Sir Geoffrey de Havilland OM, CBE, AFC, RDI; Richard M. Clarkson OBE, BSc, ACGI, FRAeS, head of the Aerodynamics department and Assistant Chief Engineer during the Comet project. He joined the company in 1925 at Stag Lane and, in 1958, was appointed Research Director of the Hatfield Division of Hawker Siddeley Aviation; Ronald E. Bishop CBE, FRAeS, who joined de Havilland in 1921 as an apprentice and took charge of the drawing office in 1936 and was responsible for the design of subsequent DH aircraft. He was appointed Special Director Hawker Siddeley Aviation 1963/64. *BAe*

rudimentary seating. The hazards were legion and the losses were serious; nevertheless the experience was invaluable to operational staff and crews who formed the mainstay of the long-haul services after the war. On 7 September 1944 BOAC operated its 1,000th Atlantic crossing, the total being doubled on 10 February 1946.

A major portion of the American manufacturing industry was fortunate in being able to concentrate upon transport aircraft, whilst in Britain, concentration was upon military aircraft in a more offensive role. Victory Aircraft of Canada, which was producing the Lancaster, converted an early Mk III to a passenger

machine by removing the turrets and fitting sheet metal fairings in their place. Trans Canada Airlines were the first operators of this very noisy nine-seater and had made 500 Atlantic crossings with its fleet of six by the end of 1945.

A later British development was the Avro York. Roy Chadwick, the designer of the Lancaster, issued the drawings for a new, slab-sided fuselage for this development of the bomber, and the prototype flew on 5 July 1942, just five months later. In 1943 three prototypes were built, one the famous *Ascalon*, Prime Minister Winston Churchill's personal transport. A minor design embarrassment in this specially appointed aeroplane was the drain from his washbasin. When the plug was removed in flight, the water, instead of running away through a drainpipe outside the fuselage, rose vertically in a fine spray! The Aeroplane and Armament Experimental Establishment at Boscombe Down directed its collective wisdom towards a solution and simply cut the end of the tube at an angle of 45° aft to induce suction in the pipe. The York was a valuable freighter which served with distinction in the 1947 Berlin Air Lift.

In America the two aircraft which were

94,95
First flown by Geoffrey Pike, on 25 September 1945, as a replacement for the Dragon Rapide, albeit a much more expensive one, the de Havilland DH104 Dove was an immediate success at a selling price of around £20,000.

Carrying up to eight passengers, it had various marks of DH Gipsy Queen engines ranging in power from 330hp to 380hp. It cruised at 162mph and the range was 1,175 miles. Many were used as company executive transports. The Dove was in production for 25 years, 542 being built.

From the Dove was developed, in response to a BEA Specification, the DH114 Heron (**95**) originally considered as the successor to the DH86B Express Airliner. The prototype was flown by Geoffrey Pike on 10 May 1950. The design accent was upon simplicity and reliability and the ability to operate from small fields. The engines were ungeared, unsupercharged 250hp Gipsy Queen 30s driving two-bladed variable pitch propellers. Hydraulics were eliminated as the undercarriage was fixed.

The Mk II Heron was fitted with a retractable undercarriage which increased speed by 20mph, to cruise at 183mph with a range of 915 miles. The Mk II was also more economical in fuel consumption, suggesting that the fixed undercarriage configuration was a mistaken economy. Many were used as executive transports, as in the case of the one shown. The ubiquitous parallel line logo cliche will be seen on the fin. Both the Queen's Flight and BEA used Herons and a total of 148 was built.

It seems surprising that, when production finished in 1963, de Havilland had no successor for the Dove or Heron or indeed the famous and very efficient Gipsy Six engine. *BAe*

96
Interior of the Heron looking forward. *BAe*

being widely used on internal and external routes were the Douglas DC-3 and the long range Douglas DC-4. Many of both types served with the US Air Force and built up a vast store of operational experience which was of value to manufacturers and operators after the war.

On 26 March 1940 the Curtiss Wright Corporation flew for the first time a new transport aeroplane which was intended as a serious competitor for the DC-3. This was the CW20 with two powerful radial engines, a pressurised cabin and an innovation in structural design — the section through the fuselage was two overlapping circles, the lower one of smaller diameter than the upper one. Where the circles intersected, the cabin floor acted as a tie between the two arcs, freight being stowed below the floor. Surprisingly it had a tailwheel undercarriage. The war prevented its development in airline service, but over 3,000 served with the American forces during hostilities. In this form it was known as the Curtiss C-46 Commando.

Boeing had developed the technically advanced B-29 bomber, chiefly remembered today as the delivery vehicle for the atom bombs dropped on Hiroshima and Nagasaki. In 1942 the USAAF ordered a transport aircraft based upon the B-29, using as many parts of that machine as possible. Towards the end of the war it was completed, and known as the XC-97. Pan American saw its potential as a passenger airliner and indicated their interest in it,

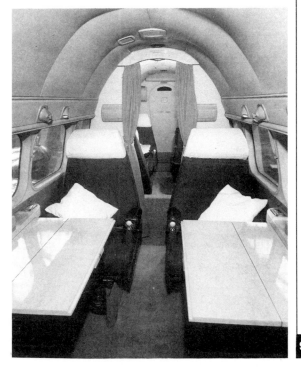

97
The Airspeed Consul was a civil conversion of surplus Oxford trainers. With seats for six passengers it was a popular postwar charter aircraft, if a somewhat noisy one with its two 395hp Armstrong Siddeley Cheetah X engines driving fixed pitch wooden propellers. Baggage was stowed in the extended nose. The all wooden airframe, originally conceived as a strengthened Envoy airframe, reveals the elegance of line characteristic of so many of Hessell Tiltman's designs. The graceful fin and rudder is well displayed in this photograph of the only Consul built as an ambulance. It cruised at 156mph and had a range of 900miles.
Airspeed Ltd

98
As an interim, indeed, hybrid airliner, the Vickers Viking must be considered a success. To produce it quickly, parts of existing Vickers aircraft were joined to a new stressed skin fuselage and the type went into service with BEA (only a month old) on 1 September 1946. The aircraft shown is painted in the BEA 'Keyline' livery, complete with the three parallel lines which seem to have been obligatory all over the world at the time. The styling cannot be seen to have much relevance to the lines of the aeroplane.

The interior was spartan and the 'usual offices' distinctly primitive. 36 passengers could be carried. Two 1,690hp Bristol Hercules engines gave the Viking a cruising speed of 263mph. The range was 1,700 miles. 163 were built.
Crown Copyright

99
Looking aft inside the Viking.
British Airways

fitted as it was with four of the Pratt and Whitney four-row radial engines which were under development. The Stratocruiser, as the new airliner was called, did not enter service until 1948.

Another outstanding American airliner which was delayed by the war was the Lockheed Constellation. First designed in 1939 to meet a Trans World Airline requirement for a long range transport, the Model 49 was larger and more powerful than its nearest competitor, the Douglas DC-4. Not until January 1943 was a prototype flown, this was the C-69 Constellation, and 150 were ordered by the USAAF as military transports. By the time

the war with Japan ended only 15 had been delivered. The remainder found a ready market among the airlines.

At the end of the war, the front runners for serious airline operations were the Douglas DC-3 and DC-4 — well proved in service — the Lockheed Constellation (a more sophisticated aeroplane than the DC-4 which was unpressurised) and the unproved Stratocruiser from the Boeing stable, albeit with a large question mark over the reliability of its immensely complicated 28-cylinder engines.

The British Avro York and Lancastrians could only be considered as stop-gap air liners. The Sunderland flying boats operated by RAF Coastal Command had triumphantly vindicated the original concept of the 'Empire' boats and, together with the three Boeing 314s operated by BOAC throughout the war, convinced many airline officials that marine aircraft had a great part to play in postwar civil aviation.

Military logistic requirements had, however, led to the construction of paved runways throughout the world. Greater independence of weather conditions had been achieved by improved air to ground communications and air traffic control methods. The Instrument Landing System and Ground Controlled Approach, developed for military use, enabled pilots to be 'talked down' in poor visibility and thus improved the safety and reliability of air services. En route navigation had benefited from the British invention of the centimetric valve, which was the basis of radar as a practical aid to navigation, although its original function was to give early warning of the approach of aircraft which might be hostile.

The future pattern of aircraft design was now becoming quite clear. All-metal stressed skin cantilever monoplanes with retractable undercarriages and flaps; carrying passengers in pressurised fuselages were to be the norm. Two or four engines driving constant speed feathering propellers were standard although there was some disagreement about the type of engine. In America radial engines were used almost exclusively, built by either Pratt and Whitney or Wright. In Britain Rolls-Royce were, of course, protagonists of the in-line, liquid-cooled engine with the Napier company building the powerful in-line Sabre, probably too complex for airline use. The famous range of Bristol radial engines designed by that master, Roy Fedden, had established their reliability in the RAF, and the relatively new sleeve valve design, with the moving poppet valves replaced by a concentric ported sleeve between the cylinder and the piston, aligning with appropriate ports in the inlet or outlet ports of the cylinder assembly, had led to the powerful Hercules twin row radial developing 2,500hp with a useful potential in postwar airliner design which had already been considered in detail as far back as 1943 when the Brabazon Committee sat to consider the possible requirements of postwar civil aviation.

Lurking quietly in the background, veiled in security, was the power unit which would revolutionise air transport. Frank Whittle had, despite enormous prejudice, received official support for his pioneering work on the gas turbine, though he was not the first engineer to study this principle. Heinkel had already flown a jet-propelled aeroplane when the Gloster E28/39 first flew on 15 May 1941. In 1944 Rolls-Royce were flying a Merlin-engined Wellington II with a Whittle turbine in the tail. Useful data was obtained from the operation of the Gloster Meteor and de Havilland

Vampire jet fighters which made their first flights with Halford designed de Havilland H1 turbines — later named Goblin — in March and September 1943, respectively.

With no modern transport aircraft in production Britain faced the years of peace with the opportunity to pioneer new aviation technology in all these related spheres, and to exercise that innovatory talent which had been manifest since the beginning of powered flight.

Britain's immediate postwar need was for interim airliners to establish a presence on the air routes of the world, whilst the recommendations of the Brabazon Committee were being turned into reality to match the powerful lead which the Americans had achieved by their concentration upon transport aircraft.

It was almost certain that, in the field of jet propulsion, Britain was well ahead of the rest of the world with de Havilland in the unique position of building a jet aeroplane, the Vampire fighter, with a Goblin engine also designed and built by the company. The de Havilland Comet was also being developed and in addition to their work on the large airliner DH was designing an aircraft to replace the Dragon

100, 101
When it became apparent, in 1945, that the Tudor would not be ready for airline service in 1946, an interim aircraft became essential. A Mk VII Halifax bomber was selected for conversion to a 12-seat machine with a large ventral pannier for freight and luggage. Twelve Handley Page Haltons went into service with BOAC for a year, after which they were sold to charter operators. With four 1,800hp Bristol Hercules engines, the Halton cruised at 260mph and had a range of 2,530 miles. As can be seen (101) the cabin furnishings were reminiscent of a barber's salon. *British Airways*

102
Britain's first jet-propelled
transport aircraft, the Vickers
Viking with Nene engines.
Rolls-Royce Ltd

103
The Avro Tudor, one of Britain's
white hopes for postwar civil
aviation, proved to be a
complete failure. The Mk 1,
illustrated in BOAC colours,
was much too small, only
accommodating 12 passengers.
There were a number of
aerodynamic problems, with
nearly 350 modifications being
made in two years, before BOAC
would accept the aircraft.
Various versions were
developed to carry more
passengers but none was
completely successful. Two
were lost on the South Atlantic
route in 1949 and the remainder
were relegated to freighter
work.
   The Tudor 4, with 1,770hp
Rolls-Royce Merlin engines,
carried up to 32 passengers at a
cruising speed of 210mph.
Range was 4,000 miles. The
clean installation of the Merlin,
with the radiator built into the
front of the nacelle is
noteworthy. A similar
installation was used on the
Canadair 4, the Merlin
conversion of the Douglas DC-4.
Only 40 Tudors were built.
From the Tudor 8 was
developed the Ashton. Fitted
with four 5,000lb thrust Rolls-
Royce Nene turbines in paired
nacelles, it was the world's first
multi-jet aircraft and was a
valuable research aircraft. It
was flown for the first time by
Capt James Orrell, Avro's chief
test pilot, who realised that he
had entered a new era of
aviation. *Aeroplane Monthly*

104
An S23 Empire flying boat being
refuelled. The vulnerability of
the hull to damage by boats is
evident. *Short Bros Ltd*

Rapide which was still giving good service
on British European Airways islands
routes.
   The new machine was the DH104 Dove,
like the Rapide, designed to carry eight
passengers. It was an all-metal structure
with many parts bonded together by the
Redux techniques originated by Dr Norman
de Bruyne whose company, Aero Research,
commenced operations at Duxford, near
Cambridge, in 1934, when he became
interested in building his own aeroplane,
the Snark. He was impressed by the simple
efficiency of wood glueing techniques
which contrasted with what he saw as the
clumsiness of riveted metal, a material
which was certain to supplant wood in
aircraft construction. He was equally sure
that a method of bonding metal would be a
very important development.
   Before the war his company pioneered
honeycomb cores and adhesives to bond
them within thin metal sheets, to form
strong and light sandwich panels. By 1941

the Royal Aircraft Establishment at
Farnborough had tested one of them and
pronounced it to be stronger than a similar
design of riveted panel.
   The de Havilland Hornet fighter of 1944
used Redux bonding in its unusual
structure. Based upon the overall design of
the Mosquito, the wings were of composite
wood and metal construction, the upper
surfaces, being subjected to compression
stresses, remained as wooden sections, but
the lower skins and members, being
subjected to a high level of stress in
tension, were made of metal, the two
materials being bonded together with
Redux under pressure and heat. The Redux
technique proved to be most satisfactory
and has been widely used in many aircraft
up to the present day.
   The Dove became a popular feeder liner
with the characteristic elegant lines of the
de Havilland marque and the well known
rudder shape. It was the first aircraft since
the Albatross to be built in its entirety by

the company, the engines were Gipsy Queen six-cylinder in line aircooled and supercharged developments of the prewar Gipsy Six, driving DH Hydromatic three-blade feathering and braking propellers — the first British airliner to have such propellers.

Six weeks after the end of hostilities in Europe, and on the 25th anniversary of the foundation of de Havilland, Geoffrey Pike flew the Dove for the first time on 25 September 1945.

The design was later stretched to increase the seating capacity from eight to a maximum of 17. This version was known as the Heron — or affectionately at Hatfield as 'Tam's Tram' — W. A. Tamblin was responsible for the design work on the conversion.

104

The measure of economic advance achieved since the days of the Dragon Rapide can be judged by the fact that the fuel consumption of the Dragon Rapide's 200hp engines and the Dove's 330hp engines was the same, at around 7½ Imperial gal/hr. It carried 150% of the Rapide's load at 125% of the speed. Gross ton-miles/gal were 27 for the Dove and 18 for the earlier machine. Payload/ton mileage was respectively 5.7 and 4.

By the end of 1946 275 Doves had been sold, a measure of the voracious appetite of world operators for this class of aeroplane backed by the company's extremely efficient and widespread service facilities.

Airspeed Ltd, by this time a wholly owned subsidiary of de Havilland, was planning a new airliner to meet one of the Brabazon recommendations. Bill Shaylor, the company's commercial director, conceived the idea of buying back RAF Oxford trainers to convert for civil use, embodying the latest civil airworthiness requirements.

The Consul, as the machine was named, was widely used by the proliferating charter firms, and was a profitable venture for Airspeed. The Avro Anson was a contemporary of the Oxford; it, too, was similarly brought up to date, mercifully with powered operation of the retractable undercarriage which, in the military version required 144 turns of a small handle to the right of the pilot's seat to raise or lower it.

Civil Airworthiness Standards were the responsibility of the Air Registration Board. First formed in 1937 to take over

105

from A&AEE at Martlesham Heath, responsibility for the certification of aeroplanes with an all-up weight of 12,500lb, it was disbanded on the outbreak of war. Towards the end of the war a Civil Test Squadron was set up at A&AEE Boscombe Down, to where the Establishment had moved in 1940. Sqn Ldr Hedley Hazelden, later to become chief test pilot of Handley Page, commanded it and was charged with the task of establishing airworthiness standards for the new breed of transports planned for production as hostilities ceased. After the war the ARB was reformed and their requirements were enshrined in the design publication *The*

105
The Saunders-Roe Princess was a 200-seat aircraft powered by ten 3,790ehp Bristol Proteus propeller turbines, eight of them being installed in the inboard nacelles coupled to drive massive four-bladed contra-rotating propellers. Three of these magnificent flying boats were to be built for BOAC, but G-ALUN, illustrated, was the only one to be completed. All three were cocooned at Cowes and Calshot and broken up in 1967. 219ft in span, the Princess would cruise at 360mph and had a range of 5,270 miles.
Aeroplane Monthly

107

106

106, 107, 108

There would probably be general acceptance of the view that, of all the piston-engined airliners built, the three most beautiful were the de Havilland Albatross, the Lockheed Constellation and the Airspeed Ambassador. Arthur E. Hagg was responsible for the design of both the British machines. The Ambassador originated in a Brabazon Committee requirement for a Dakota replacement. Hagg successfully argued that a larger machine was required. He was also convinced that two powerful engines would achieve better economic results if allied to a high degree of aerodynamic refinement. Four engines for reliability was almost a cult in those days, but Hagg convinced the Civil Aviation Authority that, provided the engines had a sufficiently high power/weight ratio to give safe single engine take-off performance, two must be better in terms of initial cost, depreciation, fuel costs, weight and maintenance.

The high aspect ratio wing allied to the superbly streamlined fuselage and engine nacelles achieved an exceptional performance. The fuselage was expensive to build but Hagg said that if the extra cost was spread over five years of operation at a utilisation of 2,000hr per annum it would be more than covered by the economic advantages of its own level of aerodynamic efficiency and the additional value of the speed achieved. Great care would be needed in skin riveting to ensure that the low drag potential of the design was realised. The success which was achieved can be seen in the photographs of G-ALZS in BEA colours.

The Centaurus powerplant had been well tested in a Vickers Warwick test bed and an innovation which achieved maximum accessibility of the

engines was the way in which the close fitting cowlings could be opened up rearwards like the petals of a flower. An electric motor provided power for hydraulic services and air conditioning so the only ground equipment necessary was a portable battery set or 'chore-horse' generating set.

After many unfortunate difficulties which delayed development, the Ambassador went into service as the 'Elizabethan' class on 13 March 1952. It was a popular aeroplane which made useful profits for BEA. The seating layout was unusual, with passengers facing forwards and aft. There was a tendency for the rearward facing ones to slide off the seat on take-off, but vibration was minimal, the traditional filled glass of water on the table remaining undisturbed.

The Elizabethans perpetuated the famous 'Silver Wing' service to Paris, inaugurated in 1927 by Imperial Airways 'Argosy' class. The all First Class cuisine was a memorable experience. The cabin interior photograph shows the 'Silver Wing' seating arrangements.

A development which, unfortunately, did not pass beyond the model stage was the Ayrshire, a freighter with loading through large clamshell doors. Twenty Ambassadors were built. The type cruised at 272mph, the range was 1,550 miles.

As a subsidiary of de Havilland, Airspeed were in a quasi-competitive position with its own parent. There is little doubt that if independent capital had been available to the company the Ambassador would have been a great British success story.
British Airways (both)

110

British Civil Airworthiness Requirements which continued to develop with the increasing complexity of aircraft.

Derived from a project to build a transport rugged enough to operate from jungle airstrips, Bristols were first in the field after the war, with their incredibly ugly but essentially practical Type 170 Freighter — called in its passenger version the Wayfarer. First flown on 2 December 1945, it was used as a workhorse all over the world and became the first car ferry when Silver City Airways began a service between Lympne in Kent and Le Touquet carrying cars in the forward hold and their passengers in a rear cabin. Car entry was through the nose section which could be swung open in two halves. The Berlin Airlift was an operation in which the type was extremely valuable.

On 22 June 1945 Vickers' 21-seat Viking airliner was flown for the first time. This

twin-engined machine had been ordered by BEA for service as quickly as possible, consequently it was a hybrid using many components of the Wellington bomber. The geodetic wings, with the engine nacelles and undercarriage, were fitted to a new metal stressed-skin fuselage. The immense strength of the structure became apparent on 13 April 1950 when a bomb exploded in the toilet of a machine flown by Capt J. Harvey and almost severed the tail. Superb flying skill brought the aircraft and passengers back safely to Northolt.

A Viking became Britain's first jet-propelled transport when it was flown with Rolls-Royce Nene engines on 6 April 1948. This machine set up a record from London to Paris in 34min 7sec on 25 July 1948, the 25th anniversary of Bleriot's crossing of the Channel. A Lancastrian was also flying with Nene engines, as a test bed, so it was possible, for the first time, to judge the merits of this new form of propulsion which greatly impressed all who experienced it.

One of Britain's white hopes was the Avro Tudor four-engined airliner. As it was from the drawing boards of the famed Roy Chadwick, great optimism was felt. It proved to be a total failure, though it was not wholly the fault of Avro. It carried only 12 passengers and was ordered by BOAC. In America the Douglas DC-4 carried 54 passengers and the Constellation, 43. A Mk 2 Tudor was projected to carry 60 passengers.

On 14 June 1945 the first Mk 1 flew with S. A. Thorn and J. H. Orrell at the controls. It was unstable and difficult to land due to the steep ground angle with the 'tail-dragger' undercarriage. On 23 August 1947 the Mark 2 was flown for the first time by Bill Thorn with Roy Chadwick as passenger. On take-off, it rolled

109
Bearing a marked resemblance to its contemporary Douglas DC-4, the chequered career of the Handley Page Hermes delayed entry of the definitive Mk IV version until August 1950 when BOAC operated its first scheduled service. In 1952 problems with systems caused their replacement by the Canadair C4 Argonaut but, in 1954, they returned to service when the Comet disasters led to the Comet fleet being grounded. Four 2,100hp Bristol Hercules engines gave a cruising speed of 276mph, the range was 2,000 miles. Up to 85 passengers could be carried. Only 25 were built. *British Airways*

110
The only Bristol Brabazon to fly. Designed by L. G. Frise and A. E. Russell, it had eight 2,500hp Bristol Centaurus engines in the wings, driving four sets of contra-rotating propellers. Its all-up weight was 290,000lb, wing span was 230ft, and the length was 177ft. Range was estimated at 5,500 miles, cruising at 250mph.

Corresponding data for the Boeing 747-200F is AUWt 836,000lb, span 195ft 8in, length 231ft 4in, range 5,120 miles cruising at 582mph, a measure of the progress made in aircraft design since the end of World War 2.
Bristol Aeroplane Co Ltd via John Stroud

111
The prototype SE161
Languedoc was first flown in
September 1945, powered by
four 1,150hp Gnome Rhône
engines. This all metal aircraft
was operated by Air France on
their European and North
African services. The machine
illustrated is one of four used in
the late 1940s for research
purposes. It carries the Leduc
0.10 ram-jet experimental
aircraft. The ram, or athodyd,
jet is a jet engine without
compressor or turbine.
Compression being achieved
solely by the ram effect of its
speed through the air,
consequently it cannot be
launched by means of its own
power. If aircraft speeds rise to
Mach 3.0 the ram-jet would
probably be used as the power
unit. *Aeroplane Monthly*

112
One of two Dart Dakotas
operated by BEA to gain
experience of the Dart before
the introduction of the
Viscount. Capt Cliff Rogers,
chief test pilot of Rolls-Royce,
administered a salutary shock
to the pilot of a Canadian Air
Force F-86 Sabre fighter who
encountered the Dak during
trials. An officer at the
Canadian base telephoned Cliff
Rogers to ask if there could be
any truth in the story quoted by
an idiot at the base that he had
seen a 'Gooney-bird', as the Dak
was affectionately known, at
36,000ft! *Rolls-Royce Ltd*

113
Originally built as a 32-seat
aircraft with four 1,380ehp Dart
propeller turbines, the
prototype Vickers Viscount first
flew on 16 July 1948. The
airlines showed no interest
until the uprating of the Dart
led Vickers to the Type 700,
which could accommodate up
to 43 passengers in the high
density configuration. BEA
ordered a fleet of them when it
became apparent, from route
trials with the small prototype,
that passengers were delighted
with the new mode of air travel.
It was also obvious that the
economics of operating the
Viscount were most
satisfactory. Illustrated is a
Type 803 which entered service
with Aer Lingus in 1966. This
version carried up to 66
passengers at a cruising speed
of 320mph; with a range of
1,200 miles. The Viscount
proved to be Britain's most
successful airliner to date, 444
being built, many of them for
overseas airlines. *Aer Lingus*

uncontrollably, crashing in a pond and killing Thorn and Chadwick. The aileron controls had been connected wrongly so that corrective action in bank only steepened the bank. Thereafter it was a requirement that the lengths of control cables should be such that it was impossible for them to be incorrectly assembled.

The Halifax bomber was converted, immediately after the war, into a 10-passenger aircraft, or as a freighter with a large pannier under the fuselage. This conversion was known as the Halton, and it became the aeronautical counterpart of the tramp steamer. The economics of it were, like those of the Lancastrian, rather disastrous.

Another first flight which ended in disaster was that of the new long range airliner from the Handley Page stable, the Hermes. On 3 December 1945 Jimmy Talbot and observer E. A. Wright took off in the new four-engined 34/45-seat Hermes from Radlett. The aircraft was seen to be following a switch back path which the pilot seemed unable to correct; it suddenly stalled and dived, inverted, to the ground, killing the crew instantly. Unbalanced elevators were said to be the cause of the disaster. Not until 2 September 1947 was Sqn Ldr Hazelden, the new chief test pilot, able to fly the second prototype, the Hermes going into service with BOAC in 1950.

An interesting exhibit at the 1948 SBAC Show at Farnborough was the Planet Satellite. Designed as a private owner's aircraft and built wholly of magnesium alloy, it had a very elegant butterfly tail and a DH Gipsy Six engine driving a pusher propeller. Unfortunately the designer's sums were incorrect. On the first taxying run one of the undercarriage legs collapsed and on a later run when the pilot, Gp Capt H. J. Wilson, lifted it into the air and landed again, the main keel member of the fuselage broke. It was not repaired. Nevertheless, it is interesting to compare it with the 1938 DH Technical School TK5 and the Edgley Optica both have a single engine driving a pusher propeller.

Short Brothers had converted a number of military Sunderlands into 'Sandringham' class passenger flying boats for operation on the BOAC long distance routes. In 1946 they were joined by the larger 'Solent' class. These set new standards of comfort and cuisine but, in 1950, the BOAC fleet was disbanded in favour of landplanes. The death knell of the marine aircraft had been sounded as soon as hard runways had been rebuilt after the war. Aquila Airways continued to fly these handsome boats on their Southampton to Madeira service until September 1950, at which time the era of the flying boat had virtually ended. At the Cowes works of Saunders Roe, however, work was proceeding on the three great 'Princess' flying 'ships', ordered for BOAC in 1946.

First flown by Geoffrey Tyson on 22 August 1958 the prototype created great interest when it was flown at the 1952 and 1953 SBAC Shows, but like its contemporary, the Brabazon, the requirement for it was an entirely fallacious one and there was no real market for either of these extremely large aircraft.

The Bristol Brabazon was designed to meet the Brabazon Committee recommendation for an airliner with the

114
With 2,400hp Pratt & Whitney engines, propellers and some instruments supplied to France under the postwar aid programme, the 12 Breguet 763 Provence airliners built for service with Air France were double-deck machines accommodating up to 135 passengers in high density configuration. A freight version had clam-shell loading doors under the rear fuselage. The cruising speed was 218mph and the range 1,345 miles. Only 16 were built, six of them being for military use. Illustrated is the prototype undergoing taxying trials — without, thanks to the censor, an undercarriage. *Aeroplane Monthly*

115, 116
A contrast in cockpit complexity. The flight deck of the 1943 L1049 Constellation and the L1649 of 1956. The half wheel on the left is for nose wheel steering. *Lockheed*

117
Constellation prototype.
Lockheed

capability of flying to New York non-stop. Eight 2,500hp Bristol Centaurus engines in coupled pairs driving counter-rotating propellers powered the monster which was flown by chief test pilot A. J. 'Bill' Pegg on 4 September 1949. There were few problems other than the sheer economics of the machine which nobody wanted. The second prototype, destined to have Proteus prop-jet engines was not completed, both were broken up.

At this time the industrial and graphic designer was being promoted by the newly formed Council of Industrial Design. One of the fashionable designers of the period was drafted to Bristol at, it was said, the behest of Prime Minister Attlee. It was his function to advise upon cabin furnishings and equipment, and Bill Pegg talked of wordy battles in the cabin mock-up. He recorded his irritation with the controversy which arose over trivia, 'I felt like saying, what the hell are you worrying about the colour of the bar, when we don't know if it will fly yet! If it does it will probably fly like a rocking horse and you won't be able to stand up, let alone drink!'

One area in which the Brabazon made a valuable contribution to the art of aircraft design was data gathering. The test pilot has the responsibility of recording every aspect of the function and performance of the machine he is testing. As it becomes larger, so the test parameters became more numerous. The Brabazon was an early example of multiple cine cameras, 12 in all, filming continuously the 1,000 dials which inform the crew and designers of the behaviour of the aeroplane and its systems.

Not all of Britain's early postwar ventures were abortive. Two outstanding aeroplanes emerged, one of which, the Airspeed Ambassador, was first flown by George Errington on 10 July 1947. This beautiful machine, designed by Arthur Hagg, the designer of the prewar DH Albatross, was originally intended to meet the Brabazon Committee requirement for a Dakota replacement. Consultation with BEA enabled Hagg to work to a higher all-up weight which would enable him to use two Bristol Centaurus engines. The high wing layout was the result of comparisons with the dimensions of a similar low wing design. The undercarriage could be shorter, therefore lighter. The advantages of having a continuous area of lift from the upper surface of the wing, and the elimination of airflow interference over the sensitive upper surface convinced the designers of the wisdom of a high wing. Passenger comfort was also enhanced by the absence of wing surface glare.

The Ambassador was to have propeller turbines installed at a later date. The Centaurus engine installation was outstandingly good from an aerodynamic and maintenance point of view, being an admirable compromise between superb streamlining and high cooling efficiency. The exhausts passed over the wing and gave extra thrust. The engine, in its 'power egg', could be changed in 17min.

Hard on the heels of the Ambassador, however, was the new Vickers liner with four Rolls-Royce Dart propeller turbines. Originally conceived as a 32-passenger airliner which first flew as the Type 630 on 16 July 1948 with 'Mutt' Summers — the veteran chief test pilot — at the controls, it set new standards of smoothness and comfort, with no vibration and little noise in the cabin. On 15 September 1949 the first Certificate of Airworthiness issued anywhere in the world for a turbine-engined aircraft was granted to the Type 630.

Work proceeded on the enlarged Type 700 with accommodation for 40 first class passengers. The prototype flew on

28 August 1950 and, from that date, the days of the Ambassador were numbered.

De Havilland was so involved in the development of its pure jet airliner that the conversion of the Ambassador to turbine power had low priority, so the type languished until it was overtaken by the Viscount, which became the most successful civil aircraft built in Britain. 459 were sold, many of them to overseas airlines.

As airports destroyed in the war were rebuilt — as a matter of high priority — in Europe and Russia, so the aircraft industries and airlines began to revive as a matter of national prestige. Various new aircraft, usually of prewar origins appeared, their orthodox construction befitting their stop-gap role. In France the Languedoc SE161 was flown in September 1945. This four-engined airliner with a tailwheel undercarriage was used by a number of operators. Its stablemate for short haul work was the SNCASO SO30 twin. Of a more modern tricycle undercarriage configuration it had a highly streamlined fuselage and, known as the Bretagne, served with Air France and other operators until the late 1950s.

In Italy the Savoia-Marchetti SM95 was revived with a larger fuselage. Initially operated by the Italian Air Force in 1943, only two of the smaller aircraft had been built by 1945 and the production run for the later version was small. Alitalia inaugurated their first international service when an SM95 flew from Rome to Oslo on 6 August 1947.

In the Soviet Union the Lisunov Li-2, or DC-3 built under licence, had been the workhorse of the military and civil transport operations. Wartime experience in aircraft design encouraged the design bureaux to consider an exclusively Russian aeroplane; one of the important

119

requirements was that it should be capable of operation from unpaved airstrips. The Ilyushin bureau produced the Il-12 which first flew in 1946. It was a good aeroplane, produced in large numbers and entered Aeroflot service in 1947.

In America Douglas flew the DC-6, a stretched DC-4, in February 1946. Originally developed for the Air Force, lack of finance caused them to lose interest, so the civil market was wide open and exploited to the full by this enterprising company.

Lockheed's new Constellation, ordered by the Air Force, was developed into a civil airliner and thus began a long period of service for this handsome aeroplane in a number of different versions which culminated in the Super Constellation of 1951. They were used on the world's long haul routes until well into the 1960s and were extremely popular with passengers.

The quest for a Dakota replacement led the Martin Company to produce the Martin 2-0-2 which first flew in November 1946. In 1948 a major wing failure caused a fatal crash and all were grounded for major modification. This disaster enabled Convair to make progress with their CV240,

118, 119
After the war production quickly switched from military to civil machines and the Lockheed Constellation was immensely popular on the air routes of the world. Originally 95ft long, 123ft in span and powered by 2,300hp Wright engines, it had a range of 3,000 miles. It was increased in length to 113ft 7in, and the L1049 series Super Constellation had, finally, 3,250hp turbo-supercharged Wright engines and could carry up to 99 passengers at a cruising speed of 355mph. Range was 4,620 miles, or as much as 6,400 miles with 58 first class passengers. During the period of development the all-up weight rose from 86,250lb to 137,000lb.

KLM bought L1049Cs which began the Amsterdam-New York service in August 1953.

The photograph of the Lufthansa L1049G (**118**) shows the beautiful lines of the aircraft, lines which presented severe difficulty in the stretching process. As well as giving extra fuel capacity the pinion tanks on the wing tips reduce bending loads on the wings and have an aerodynamic advantage in reducing airflow around the tip from the lower to the upper surfaces. The superb styling of the Lufthansa livery cleverly enhances the shape of the Constellation and the famous 1919 vintage flying crane is an attractive emblem of dateless character.

The interior view (**119**) shows a tourist class interior commissioned by TWA for their L1049s.

Over 200 Constellations of all types were built — it must be considered as one of the world's classic aeroplanes.
Lockheed; Lufthansa

Postwar American Airliners

120-122

The Douglas DC-4 (**120**) went
into production in 1941 and
was widely used by the
American forces as a military
transport. Douglas was
therefore in a strong position to
meet the urgent postwar need
for a civil airliner with this
modern and well proven design,
powered by four 1,450hp Pratt
& Whitney Twin Wasp engines.
The US Government sold or
leased about 500 of the military
versions to civilian operators
and Douglas sold a further 79.
44 passengers could be carried
at a cruising speed of 280mph;
range was 2,500 miles. The
DC-4 was the first airliner to be
built with a constant diameter
section fuselage. This enabled
it to be 'stretched' easily and in
1946 the DC-6 (**121**) was
produced with a pressurised
cabin to accommodate up to 102
passengers in a high density
fuselage, 7ft longer. The
engines were 2,400hp Twin
Row Wasps which increased
the cruising speed to 315mph
and the range to 3,005 miles.
Over 500 variants of the DC-6
were built.

Also in 1946, Canadair, who
were building DC-4s, produced
the Canadair 4, later known as
the North Star. As Merlin
engines could be imported
without financial penalties
these engines were used. The
usual prominent Merlin
radiators were neatly included
in the cowling profile giving the
installation the appearance of a
radial engine. The cabin was
pressurised, carrying 40 first
class or 62 economy class
passengers. The cruising speed
was 289mph and the range
3,880 miles.

The final development of this
outstanding aeroplane was the
DC-7 (**122**) which appeared in
1953. Powered by four turbo-
supercharged 3,250hp Wright
radial engines, the DC-6
fuselage was stretched to
accommodate a further row of
seats. The wing span remained
at 117ft 6in. The increased
engine power gave a cruising
speed of 359mph but the range
was reduced to 2,850 miles.

The later DC-7B, with
increased fuel to enable it to fly
the Pan Am route to Europe
could not fly directly in the
westerly direction against
strong winds. The DC-7C was
built to enable the service to be
independent of wind problems.
Span was increased by 10ft to
enable more fuel to be carried

(continued)

to a similar specification. The Martin aircraft developed into the 3-0-3 and 4-0-4, of increased size, the 4-0-4 having a pressurised cabin. The Convair CV240 was pressurised from the outset and was the first commercial aeroplane to use in its structure what is now known as a composite material. The trailing edges of the rudder and elevators were formed sections of glass reinforced plastic.

The Pratt and Whitney Wasp engines had an ingenious form of exhaust system. The exhausts were two large tubes projecting **123** from the rear of the nacelle, which entrained cooling air as it passed over the engines and decreased cooling drag, at the same time generating a measure of extra thrust. Unfortunately the system was noisy. The Convair 240 was a popular transport aircraft and some are still flying today.

In 1951 the French firm of Breguet flew for the first time its four-engined Br763 Provence. Originally it was not favoured by Air France, but in 1951 an improved and more powerful version was produced; Air France ordered 12 of these large double deck aircraft which could carry 135 passengers.

By the end of the decade aircraft systems were becoming complicated. It was apparent that the transport aircraft of the future must have power operated controls and not rely upon the physical strength of the pilot, aided by aerodynamic balancing, to control the aeroplane. The Boulton Paul Aircraft Company at Wolverhampton was among the pioneers, and chief test pilot A. E. 'Ben' Gunn, had already flown many hours in a Lancaster fitted with powered controls. High altitude flying during the war had proved that the carbon brush type of current generator was useless, the brush wear being excessive; however the development of an alternating current brushless generator solved this problem and offered scope for a large electrical load to be provided for the services needed, particularly in the avionics, or aviation electronics, area of consumption.

Navigational aids were becoming more efficient, and the need for a separate navigator in the crew was almost eliminated.

Structural design had become relatively straightforward although the housing of fuel was a difficult problem. The voracious thirst of the powerful engines available

meant that every available cubic inch of space must be used. This meant that separate tanks were no longer practicable. Bag tanks which were pushed into the wing structure were an improvement but the real answer was to use the whole of the wing interior as a tank. This introduced difficult problems of sealing the structure. In practice, the fuel carrying area is usually the wing between the forward and rear spars, so the main stress on the sealants occurs under bending loads rather than the much more difficult torsional loads. Varying temperatures from hot to extremely cold will be experienced and pressures too will vary considerably.

Hydraulic systems were well understood and most reliable, although working pressures were high at 3,000lb/sq in.

Cabin air conditioning was a complex art riddled with problems, the physiological aspect of the crew and passenger environment was important and valuable work had been carried out during the war by the RAF Institute of Aviation Medicine. The magnitude of the difficulties encountered is illustrated by the disaster which occurred to an American airliner in the 1950s; in flight, the cabin air heater, petrol fuelled, suddenly ejected sheets of flame into the cabin, and all aboard died in the ensuing crash.

It will be apparent that the designers of civil aircraft in the next few decades had a formidable armoury of technology to direct torwards the unknown problems which would be faced, problems which began when the de Havilland DH106 Comet thrilled the aviation world as Gp Capt John Cunningham, the chief test pilot, flew this beautiful aeroplane for the first time on 27 July 1949.

It was the harbinger of the jet age and will be considered in the next chapter.

and, as the engines were moved outboard, noise in the cabin was reduced. The DC-7C, or Seven Seas as it became known, had a range of 2,850 miles, the cruising speed remaining at 359mph.

It is probably true to say that the DC-6 was stretched too far in the case of the DC-7. The complex engines were troublesome, and the arrival of the Boeing 707 was imminent as the last of them was in production. They made a major contribution, however, in flying non-stop commercial flights over the Atlantic and Pacific oceans, over the North Pole and across the American continent. 388 of the type were built. *American Airlines; Aeroplane Monthly; Pan Am*

123
Consolidated-Vultee, later known as Convair, produced its Dakota replacement, the CV240, which first flew in March 1947. From this was developed the stretched CV340 in 1951 and in 1955 the CV440 Metropolitan was launched when the impact of the Vickers Viscount on American airlines became apparent. Many overseas airlines operated the Metropolitan, including Swissair. The clean lines and high aspect ratio wing is apparent in the photograph. The engine exhaust is a rectangular orifice at the rear of the nacelle. The CV240 was one of the first airliners to have a built-in loading stair below the rear of the cabin. The CV440 had an air stair built in on the port side, forward of the wing. Fitted with 2,500hp Pratt & Whitney engines, the CV440 had a cruising speed of 300mph and a range of 285 miles at full load, reflecting the short-haul function for which it was designed. It could seat up to 52 passengers. Over 1,000 CV240/340/440 liners were built. *Swissair*

6

Into the Jet Age

124
The Bristol 171 Sycamore was designed by Raoul Hafner as a four-seat helicopter powered by a 450hp Wright Whirlwind engine. It first flew in July 1947 and received the first Certificate of Airworthiness to be issued to a British helicopter. The Mk 2 version with an Alvis Leonides was flown in September 1949. On its second attempt to take off the rotor disintegrated, luckily at low altitude so it merely fell back on to the grass just as Bill Pegg was leading a group of journalists away from the Brabazon after a demonstration flight. Noticing this unseemly occurrence, Pegg made the memorable remark, 'Oh, that's just a routine test!' and walked on.

This uniquely elegant helicopter had a cruising speed of 132mph and a range of 330 miles. 180 were built.
British Airways

125
One of BOAC's Boeing Stratocruisers. This giant airliner set high standards of comfort in its double-deck accommodation, with its 'double bubble' fuselage. A spiral staircase led to a smart bar or lounge on the lower deck. BOAC operated 10 Stratocruisers, named after the 'C' class Empire flying boats. Up to 100 passengers could be carried. With four 3,500hp Pratt & Whitney engines, the 141ft 3in span machine could cruise at 340mph and had the impressive range of 2,750 miles. The square tipped propellers, of large diameter to absorb the power, were of hollow steel construction.

The Stratocruiser was the first BOAC aircraft to have a white cabin top, an innovation introduced by Pan American in 1946 to lower the cabin temperature of airliners standing in hot sunshine. This simple and effective idea was widely adopted and gave the paint scheme designers a valuable visual feature. 55 Stratocruisers were built.
BOAC

For several years after the European war had ended, the airlines were facing many difficulties in consolidating their position. Many airports had been rebuilt after the ravages of bombing raids, but few of them remained on their original sites near the cities they served. London was an example. Croydon had no runways and was bordered by housing estates — insurmountable problems. Commercial operations began from RAF Northolt, west of London, which had paved runways and limited administration facilities, including Customs. BEA made its base here, whilst BOAC used Hurn, near Bournemouth, for the Atlantic and Empire services. The experience of the North Atlantic which had been gained on the Return Ferry Service was invaluable to the airline. During its four years of operation, about 1,750 crossings had been made, carrying 20,000 passengers, 1,000 tons of mail and 600 tons of freight.

BOACs flying boat services operated from Poole Harbour. An interesting development in 1947 was the establishment of a BEA helicopter unit with a Westland S51 and two small Bell machines. The unit also showed interest in the new Bristol Sycamore helicopter, the earliest helicopter to show aesthetic, as well as technical, merit.

The 1948 blockade of Berlin by the Russians, and the successful air lift to relieve the city, was a remarkable proving ground for techniques of traffic control for an immense volume of different aeroplanes — techniques which were refined in later years as air traffic grew.

The potentialities of automatic flight had been effectively demonstrated in 1947 when a Douglas C-54A of the US Army All Weather Flying Centre landed at RAF Brize Norton, having flown from the USA under auto-control. Before the Atlantic crossing the pilot switched on the engine and flying control servos and 'flew the beam' purely as an observer. Automatic control of height, speed and let-down was achieved. As the machine touched down, the compression of the undercarriage oleo legs closed the throttles, the pilot, then, taking control.

In Britain the Royal Aircraft Establishment had formed a Blind Landing Experimental Unit (BLEU) at RAF Woodbridge in Suffolk and considerable progress had been made in developing techniques which, as early as January 1945, allowed an RAE Boeing 247D to land at RAF Defford in complete darkness with no landing lights and with all other lighting obscured by the wartime black-out restrictions. There was no flare-out, the low approach speed and shallow glide enabled the machine to fly straight on to the ground. It is believed that this was the world's first automatic landing.

In 1949 a demonstration was given of the various elements of an automatic landing system in different aircraft used for testing them. The well proved ILS system and a

radio altimeter were the foundations of the equipment, with twin leader cables guiding the aircraft to the runway in a level position. Standard autopilots, which had been developed during the war, were replaced by a new Smiths Industries design of all-electric autopilot. Progress was stimulated by the acceptance of the SCS51 Instrument Landing System as an international standard, and also by the work carried out at RAE Farnborough by E. S. Calvert on approach and runway lighting systems.

It was possible to accept ILS as a radio guide down to 150ft, when the pilot would take over to land manually by visual guidance from the Calvert centreline and crossbar lighting which has now been developed for use as a worldwide standard.

The difficult problem of automatic flare-out remained to be solved as did the crucial one of reliability. The use of multiple elements with the automatic switching out of a suspect unit ultimately achieved a system which is now widely used for airline operations. The dedicated work of the BLEU test pilots cannot be praised too highly; the continual 'circuits and bumps' necessary to prove the complex equipment must have been extremely boring. The unit ultimately moved to RAE Bedford.

The Boeing Stratocruiser was fitted with a device which was an early element in the automation of the flightdeck; an engine condition analyser informed the pilot or flight engineer of fuel or ignition malfunctions and as soon as the 60 ton airliner touched down, the inboard propellers moved automatically into reverse pitch. The Stratocruiser also introduced to BOAC the first electronic flightdeck simulator to reduce costs in crew training.

Various synthetic devices had been built since 1917, but it was not until 1936 that the American Edwin Link produced his famous trainer familiar to thousands of pilots in the 1930s and 40s. A vestigial fuselage was mounted on bellows, and would move in relation to the control input by the pilots. Later versions had a 'crab' marker travelling over a chart on the plotting table so that navigation training could take place. A modern version of this type is in production by Singer Link-Miles at Lancing in Sussex.

The British Telecommunications Research Establishment built a number of

125

126

127

126
The world's first fully electronic simulator. Built by Rediffusion Ltd for British Overseas Airways to train crews of the Boeing Stratocruiser in 1951. *Rediffusion Simulation Ltd*

127
Sir George R. Edwards CBE, DSc, Hon FRAeS, Hon FAIAA, joined Vickers Armstrongs Ltd at Weybridge in 1935, became Chief Designer in 1945 and a Special Director in 1948. He was responsible for the Viking, Viscount, Valiant bomber, the VC10 and the BAC 1-11. He was awarded the Daniel Guggenheim Medal in 1959. *Aeroplane Monthly*

128
An SAS Douglas DC-9-71 in the new livery of the airline. Note the national colours of the three participating countries below the cabin window and their heraldic shields on the engine nacelle. *SAS*

128

129
Douglas DC-6B *Arild Viking* after its flight from USA over the North Pole. Note the stylised dragon termination of the fuselage colour line. *SAS*

130
In the early days of the Comet project, the de Havilland designers thought that a swept-wing tail-less configuration would be a feasible solution to the problems of high speed flight so the DH108 Swallow was built. On 6 September 1948 it became the first British aircraft to fly faster than sound. Piloted by John Derry this flight was part of an extremely hazardous series of tests he carried out exploring the transonic regime which had already killed his predecessor, Geoffrey de Havilland, when his DH108 disintegrated over the Thames Estuary in September 1946. Instability in pitch proved to the company that such a radical departure from the orthodox configuration was not feasible in the light of contemporary knowledge. *BAe*

different systems trainers for the Services during the war.

Curtiss-Wright, in America, introduced the computer into simulation, and received an order from Pan American Airways for a unit to reproduce the aerodynamic, engine control and aircraft handling characteristics of their new Stratocruisers. This was delivered in 1948, and Pan Am was soon able to announce a reduction of 60% in crew training costs. There was no 'motion system' in this early device so, to that extent, it lacked true realism.

The BOAC simulator was built in UK by Redifon Ltd, at a cost of £100,000, it was calculated that it would save £90,000 per year in training costs. Since that time the development of flightdeck simulation has reached extraordinary levels of realism with the airfield which the aircraft is approaching being shown in front of the pilot.

By 1950 that sea of mud known as London Airport was operating from three runways, with primitive accommodation for staff and passengers. Four runways remained to be completed, and work had commenced on the central terminal building which was located within the area bounded by the runways — a scheme which has caused many problems in developing the airport. Indeed it has caused Terminal Four to be built a considerable distance from the other three.

The world's first long range radar surveillance system — a British invention — was installed, and air traffic control over Britain was exercised through five flight information regions.

Poor visibility approaches were carried out by a technique pioneered by the RAF during the war — Ground Controlled Approach (GCA). The ground controller watched the approaching aircraft on his cathode ray displays, and gave the pilot a running commentary of speed, altitude and headings to position him exactly on the glide path. When he was about 2½ miles from the runway threshold he would be warned to check undercarriage and flaps; 400yds from touch down he would be instructed 'Look ahead for landing'. It required immense faith in the controller on the part of the pilot.

1951 was the year of the prestigious and exciting Festival of Britain, mainly concentrated in London at the South Bank site and at Battersea. Both the national airlines featured the Festival in their

publicity, some of the best of which came
from the studio of Abram Games, one of the
leading graphic designers of the period,
who had himself designed much of the
graphics at the sites.

The year 1951 also saw the beautiful
de Havilland Comet on route proving trials
which showed what true 'over the weather'
flying was like. The sensation of sitting
motionless in space with a dark blue sky
above was commented upon by many
observers.

The Vickers Viscount 630 prototype was
also well advanced in its flight trials under
'Mutt' Summers and 'Jock' Bryce.

On 26 July 1950, G-AHRF, as the
prototype was registered, was awarded a
full Certificate of Airworthiness. Three
days later, it took off in BEA colours, flown
by BEA captain 'Dicky' Rymer, on the
world's first scheduled service by such an
aircraft. It carried 14 fare-paying
passengers and 12 guests, including Sir
Alec Coryton, of the Ministry of Supply,
George Edwards, the designer of the
aircraft, Sir Frank Whittle and Peter
Masefield, the chief executive of British
European Airways.

The quietness of the cabin and complete
freedom from vibration made a deep
impression on all the passengers and the
journalists aboard wrote enthusiastically
about the opening of a new era in
commercial aviation. The large oval
windows were a popular feature. The
230-mile trip from Northolt to Paris took
57min.

On 3 August BEA ordered 20 of the
enlarged Type 701 Viscounts and launched
the career of the most successful
commercial aircraft ever built in Britain
and certainly one of the most delightful to
travel in. It was a classic design with a
classic engine.

Safety was a major feature in the new
breed of turbine aircraft, highly volatile
aviation spirit was unnecessary, as
kerosene was used; however, the cruising
speeds were rising fast, the Comet to
almost 500mph and the Viscount to
324mph. Risk of collision at high closing
speeds was serious, and turbulence at
those speeds was a potential hazard to the
structural integrity of the airframe.

BOAC formed a special Development Unit
to work on the problem of detecting high
ground or approaching aircraft, and the
presence of cloud likely to be menacing.
E. K. Cole Ltd produced a collision warning
radar which was tested in Vikings at Hurn

131
DH106 Comet I G-ALYP leaving
Heathrow on 2 May 1952 on the
world's first scheduled
commercial flight by a jet-
propelled aeroplane. This
triumph turned to tragedy on
10 January 1954 when 'Yoke
Peter' disintegrated over the
Mediterranean, near Elba,
followed soon afterwards by a
second one. Both disasters were
found to have been caused by a
fatigue failure in the skin of the
fuselage.

The magnitude of the
problems likely to be
experienced with the operation
of this revolutionary airliner at
twice the speed and altitude of
current transports had led
de Havilland to one of the most
comprehensive series of
functional tests ever carried out
upon an aeroplane. The first
production wing was attached
to a section of fuselage and
subjected, by means of
hydraulic rams, to deflection
tests over a range of 3ft, these
were carried out thousands of
times. Landing loads were
applied to the undercarriage
assemblies and 16,000
retractions were made with the
bearings packed with grease
and sand. The nose wheel
steering was tried out by
mounting the nose wheel, with
pilot's wheel, on a three-ton
truck chassis which was driven
at speeds up to 50mph for 120
miles.

A chamber was built at
Hatfield to test components in
cold, rarified air, to limits of
−70°C and the equivalent of an
altitude of 70,000ft. Sections of
the fuselage were tested to
pressures up to 200% of the
normal cabin pressure of
8.75lb/sq in. Sadly, the whole
fuselage was not tested in this
way in its entirety. If this had
been done, hindsight tells us
that the story of the Comet
would have been a very
different one. *British Airways*

132
The first jet airliner simulator
was designed for the Comet 1
by Rediffusion. The illustration
shows the later Comet 4
simulator with limited 'motion'
capability. *British Airways*

133
Boeing originally considered powering the Stratocruiser with propeller turbines to meet the postwar market requirements but the success of the DH Comet, which flew five years before the 707, convinced the company that a pure jet transport was required. The B-47 Stratojet bomber contributed aerodynamic data and the lessons learned from the Comet disasters were made available to Boeing. The outcome was the 707 — an outstanding airliner which remained in production for 25 years. On 19 October 1959 Pan Am commenced its scheduled trans-Atlantic service with what was the first true long-haul jet. The photograph shows one of BOAC's 707s in its smart dark blue and white livery. In a period of innovation and experiment one particularly nasty refinement for air travellers was the use of background music in the passenger cabin. The author recalls sitting in a 707 at Heathrow waiting to take off for Sydney. The choice of music was, perhaps unfortunate, 'The Lord High Executioner' from 'The Mikado'!

Over 800 of the type were built, most will go out of service in 1986 when new international noise level regulations come into force.

134
Lufthansa catering. *Lufthansa*

135
The Douglas DC-8 closely resembled the Boeing 707, but with only 30° of sweepback on the wing. The type entered airline service with Delta and United in September 1959, 11 months after the 707. This fact, together with the greater flexibility of the Boeing, which could be supplied in different fuselage lengths, handicapped Douglas sales. Nevertheless, the DC-8 was a fine aircraft and deservedly popular. On 14 March 1966 the Series 61 first flew. This had been stretched by an incredible 36ft 8in to seat up to 259 passengers. With four 18,000lb thrust Pratt & Whitney turbines its cruising speed was 580mph and the range was 4,300 miles. About 400 of the variants, including freighters were built. *McDonnell Douglas*

134

and in 'Hythe' class flying boats. It was used operationally in some of BOAC's Hermes IVs in 1950. The radar set could detect cloud, coastlines or mountains at a distance of 40 miles and an approaching aeroplane of airliner size at 10 miles.

During the war, high flying test pilots in jet-propelled Meteors had reported serious turbulence in clear air. Meteorologists disbelieved them initially, but, ultimately, they had to accept that such phenomena existed. This hazard is a product of jet-streams which flow generally in westerly latitudes, at speeds in excess of 80mph. Their presence cannot be detected until the aircraft enters them, when the passengers feel as though they are travelling over cobble stones. Pilots were instructed to change altitude to avoid exposure to clear air turbulence which could impose serious stresses and could not be detected by radar.

It will be apparent that, by 1950, the infrastructure for a massive expansion of civil aviation existed. Efficient, reliable airliners were available, a number of which had been proved in the exacting service of war. The flying boat, said in 1928 'to carry its airport on its bottom' was about to be phased out by BOAC. The proliferation of paved runways throughout the world relegated these magnificent aircraft to increasingly uneconomic operation by enthusiasts for enthusiasts — but only for another decade or so.

Two-class travel was a reality, and IATA directed its attention to one of its less desirable projects, one which did nothing to improve the lot of the non-First Class passenger. Standards were established for seat pitch and in-flight catering. The increasing volume of passengers introduced problems for the galley. The 'First Class' syndrome seemed inherent in the airline operators thinking. Some tried to feed passengers on the ground, others thought that boredom would be lessened by serving them in the air. Not until deep frozen food was introduced was it possible to pre-cook the food, store it at a very low

135

136
A Swissair CV990 Coronado showing the streamlined fairings fitted above the wing to overcome the drag problems discovered during the flight test programme which began in 1961, 6½ years after the Boeing 707. The aerodynamic problems delayed the Coronado's entry into Swissair service until March 1962. Four 16,050lb thrust General Electric CJ805 turbofans gave this graceful aircraft a cruising speed of 556mph, with a range of 3,800 miles. Only 37 were built. The Spanish charter firm, Spantax, bought 14 and operated some of them well into the 1980s.
Swissair via John Stroud

137
The Caravelle, first flown in May 1955, was the world's first short/medium range jet airliner and, as such, confounded the pundits who were convinced that the pure jet engine was totally uneconomic for other than long haul services. It was the first jet aircraft to have the engines at the tail, and the tailplane was mounted on the fin to avoid buffeting from the jet efflux. The aerodynamic advantages of leaving the wing free of excrescences such as engine nacelles or pylon mountings were substantial and the effect upon cabin noise levels was remarkable, particularly for those in the front of the cabin.

The production Caravelle 1, with Rolls-Royce Avon engines, carried 64 passengers in mixed class seating. The final development of this handsome aircraft was the Mk 12 with Pratt & Whitney turbofans. Only 12 of these were built out of a production total of 280. It carried a maximum of 140 passengers cruising at 513mph; the range was 2,510 miles. The Caravelle was operated by 35 airlines and some are still flying with charter companies.
Aeroplane Monthly

138
The Bristol Britannia stemmed from a 1947 requirement for a medium range airliner. Bristol's design carried 48 passengers with four Centaurus engines and two were built. Later the design was stretched for long haul routes to carry 139 passengers — four Proteus turboprops were used, each developing 4,120ehp giving a cruising speed of 355mph. Range was 4,100 miles and 45 of this version were built, the type being overtaken by the 707.

The Britannia was a very comfortable aeroplane, popular with its passengers and airport neighbours, the noise levels from the Proteus engines being commendably low.

In 1954 Canadair negotiated a licence to build a version of the Britannia for the Royal Canadian Air Force. It finally emerged as a civilian freighter, the CL44D-4 with four Rolls-Royce Tyne propeller turbines developing 5,730ehp each. The CL44D-4 was the first aeroplane in the world with the whole of the tail hinged to allow large loads to be driven straight into the capacious hold.

The photograph of the Britannia in flight shows the elegant lines to advantage, lines enhanced by the smart BOAC livery of the period. The cabin top, fin and rudder were white, with 'cheat lines' and Speedbird emblem were in dark blue, the rest of the surfaces were in a natural polished metal finish.
British Airways

139

139
Deflection tests on the port wing of a Britannia shown by sequential exposure. The lower exposure shows the wing in its static, unloaded position, the centre one at proof load (the load which the structure must withstand, and remain serviceable) whilst the upper exposure shows the deflection of nearly 7ft to 95% of its ultimate load (ie on the verge of structural failure). *BAE*

temperature and then take it aboard the aircraft to be de-frosted and heated.

IATA defined precisely the meals which could be provided for non-First Class travellers. Later, in 1957, seat pitch was specified at a maximum of 34in, except for reasons of safety.

The aircraft designers were producing aeroplanes capable of reducing substantially time in the air; the time wasted at the airports, and in travelling to and from them, was not being reduced. Indeed, the increasing volume of passengers was likely to worsen the problems of embarkation, Customs clearance and baggage handling. Airport designers and builders of such equipment as fuellers, galley and toilet servicing vehicles, luggage handlers and, above all, embarkation facilities were forced to consider deeply the needs of the passengers. Unfortunately, at most large

airports, it seems that passenger growth has always exceeded the capacity to process them to their destinations. A case, perhaps, of the path to Hell being paved with good intentions.'

A powerful influence upon the postwar airline scene was the formation in 1946 of Scandinavian Airline Systems, usually known as SAS. This amalgamation of the Danish, Swedish and Norwegian airlines DDL, ABA and DNL, led to consideration of a new air route from Scandinavia to the US West Coast across the North Pole. There were problems, as the aircraft would fly over vast tracts of uninhabited territory with no radio beacons, and the necessity of, perhaps, two refuelling stops under conditions which were unfamiliar and hostile to passengers, most crews and, to a degree, the aeroplanes themselves.

Navigation was difficult, map reading in the vicinity of the North Pole meant that meridians would be crossed so often that the true heading changed more frequently than the navigator could calculate. A new projection of parallel lines was designed to be superimposed upon a plotting chart, virtually eliminating, in effect, the North Pole. Not so easily eliminated was the major problem in Polar navigation — the loss of direction of a magnetic compass and the fact that the Magnetic North Pole moves northwest at about five miles each year. A directional gyro seemed to be the answer, but, as the earth is also slowly rotating, there is an apparent drift which is at its maximum at the Pole.

The American Bendix Corporation and SAS solved the problem with the Polar Path Gyro. Using this, the navigator sets for the latitude flown as the instrument reduces the drift component to almost zero. The navigator's periscopic sextant is useless at

those latitudes because of the 24hr Arctic sun in the summer and the fact that even when it disappears below the horizon in spring and autumn, it still has enough power to obscure the stars. Another American invention, the Kollsman Sky Compass, permitted him to take a fix on the sun when it was below the horizon.

SAS also had to build radio stations along the route and devise survival gear for the occupants of the aircraft in the event a forced landing in these inhospitable regions. Padded clothing, sleeping bags, snow shoes, an Eskimo dictionary, rubber rafts, emergency rations, traps, fishing gear and guns were in the inventory.

The airline ordered the Douglas DC-6B for its long haul routes. In November 1952 the first aircraft, *Arild Viking* made a proving flight over the route from the Douglas plant in California to Copenhagen, stopping at Edmonton, Canada and Thule, in Greenland.

The American carriers feared that traffic was likely to be drawn from their services and it was not until 1954 that permission was received to go ahead. The Trans-Polar route is now commonplace, but the navigator is no longer a member of the crew. He has been replaced by the Inertial Navigation System which controls the whole operation to a remarkable degree of accuracy from take off to landing, with no intermediate stop.

SAS has been a significant influence in the aesthetics of air transport; the traditional talent of the Scandinavian nations in the field of decoration and design has produced an elegant house style which has developed since 1946 when the Viking dragon, with the three national flags and the striking treatment of the name of the line over the windows was seen on the first Douglas DC-4 Skymaster to go into service. The aircraft interiors are attractive in soft colours so well known to visitors to these northern countries whilst the charm of the smartly dressed stewardesses and the crews of the aircraft set enviably high standards.

The importance which SAS attributes to 'corporate identity', as 'house style' has come to be known, is apparent from the fact that, when a new corporate identity programme was launched in 1983, a 24-page colour brochure was produced to explain and illustrate the whole concept as it affected every aspect of the operation. **141**

The general style is most attractive, but there may be doubts about the wisdom of replacing the dragon with a group of national colours in stripes at an angle below the forward cabin window. They create a jagged interruption of the flowing line of the aeroplane whereas the Viking dragon complemented the line.

To revert to the technical scene of the early 1950s, BOAC operated its first — indeed, the world's first — jet-propelled passenger service with a de Havilland Comet I on 2 May 1952 when G-ALYP — Yoke Peter, later to be the first tragic victim of the fatigue problem which beset the Comet I — left Heathrow for Johannesburg.

Boeing had decided that the success of the Comet threatened their leading position, with Douglas, in the airline market. Their response was to build a military tanker which would give them a good production run to help amortise the heavy tooling costs, this machine, in airliner form would be the American answer to the formidable Comet.

The prototype Boeing 707 was flown for the first time on 15 July 1954, having been delayed by an unfortunate undercarriage failure. In common with the Comet, it had a

140
Freight being loaded aboard a Canadair CL44 of BOAC.
British Airways

141
The Lockheed Electra was another casualty of the rapid transition to the pure jet era. First flown in December 1957 it went into service in January 1959 powered by Allison turboprop engines of 3,750ehp each. Two fatal accidents in mysterious circumstances caused restrictions to be placed upon operating speeds. Resonance problems, leading to structural failure, were identified and cured by January 1961, but by that time it was too late. The type was overtaken by the jets. The Electra was later developed into the P-3 Orion, the US Navy's very successful maritime reconnaissance aircraft.

The passenger version, L188C, carried up to 99 passengers at a cruising speed of 405mph. Range was 2,500 miles. 170 Electras were built.
Lockheed

142
The prototype of the Fairey Rotodyne. *British Airways*

143
A 6,000gal Pluto tanker refuelling a Pan Am DC-7C at London airport in 1957. *Esso*

swept wing which, it was now realised, was essential for flight approaching the speed of sound, known as Mach One after the German physicist who studied supersonic flight in depth. There the similarity ended. De Havillands decided to build the four DH Ghost turbines into the wing roots, partly to avoid asymmetric thrust problems in the event of an engine failure, and partly to permit a thin wing, so necessary to achieve minimum drag.

Boeing decided to follow a most unusual course by mounting the engines in pods underneath the wing, thus reducing airflow interference to the minimum and also, by locating them well outboard, reducing the bending loads upon the wing structure. Different engines could be accommodated easily and their maintenance was facilitated by easy access.

The outcome of the official enquiry into the Comet disasters was made available to Boeing, the 707 benefiting from the findings. Airline pilots who flew it liked the machine which was ordered by Pan Am. Passengers noted the small cabin windows, a reflection of the problem of high pressure differentials between the cabin interior and the outside. The prototype was underpowered so water injection into the combustion chambers was used for take-off. One wag, reputedly from Hatfield, said 'The only thing that gets the 707 into the air is the curvature of the earth!' Nevertheless the 707 became an extremely good aeroplane, particularly after the Air Registration Board had studied it from the viewpoint of certification for service on BOAC's routes. David P. Davies, who later became chief test pilot of ARB, was entrusted with this project. He liked the new machine but was unhappy with its 'dutch roll' characteristics. This is a form of instability in which the aeroplane rolls and yaws simultaneously from side to side. On training flights with an engine out there were occasions when the first production 707s dutch-rolled so violently that engines were torn away from the wing. ARB insisted upon various modifications, including a small fin extension under the fuselage. Boeing was so impressed with the result of this increase in fin area that an enlarged fin and rudder was made a formal retro-fit kit to be added to 707s in service.

Flying controls had become a major technical development area with the new jets in the 1950s. It had been proved by various test pilots, such as Geoffrey de Havilland and John Derry, that powered controls were absolutely essential for high speed aircraft. They had to be irreversible and entirely free of the results of wear inevitable with the many pin joints in manual systems. Power control required the introduction of 'feel', so that the pilot had a sensory response to the loads he was

applying to the aircraft by the movement of the controls. Without this feature it would have been easy to overstress the airframe to an excessive degree. The high loading of the swept wings of sub-sonic aircraft required the development of extremely complex high lift devices if take-off and landing distances and speeds were to remain within acceptable limits. The 707 was an early example of this trend; on the approach to land the after surface of the wing appeared to be hydraulically 'dismantled', two sets of slotted flaps moving aft and downwards whilst full span flaps moved downward at the leading edge of the wing to form a blunt, high lift profile.

144
The 1985 version of the British Aerospace 748 which has proved to be one of Britain's most successful exports. Out of a total of 475 civil and military aircraft, 316 were sold abroad. With two Rolls-Royce Dart Mk 552 prop turbines of 2,280eshp each, the 748 can carry 48 passengers at a seat/mile cost which is claimed to be lower than that of any other 44-56 seat turboprop aircraft. Low noise levels have been achieved, partly by a new system of dynamic balancing of the propellers to high standards of accuracy. *BAe*

145
Interior of the BAe 748. *BAe*

145

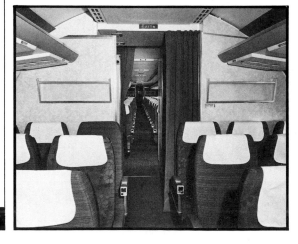

146

146-148
First flown by Group Captain
John Cunningham on 9 January
1962, the Trident was a most
advanced aeroplane, with three
9,850lb thrust Rolls-Royce Spey
turbines with thrust reversers
on the outboard engines. The
machine had an impressive
performance. The wing was
swept 35° and was equipped
with a comprehensive range of
high lift devices to ensure
safety of operation from normal
length runways. This was
particularly important as it was
designed from the outset for
automatic landing, and was,
indeed, the first aeroplane in
the world to be certificated as
such. The undercarriage was
unusual in that the nosewheel
retracted sideways and was
offset 2ft from the centre line to
achieve this.
(**146**)HRH the Duke of
Edinburgh is seen at the
controls of a Trident; (**147**) the
cabin interior; (**148**) the Mk 3B
— stretched to carry up to 180
passengers, the wings were
enlarged and, to achieve a
satisfactory take-off
performance, an extra 5,250lb
thrust jet was fitted at the tail
as can be seen in the
photograph which shows one of
a number of Tridents, including
3Bs, sold to the Chinese
national airline, CAAC. The Mk3
had a cruising speed of 581mph
and a range of 1,094 miles. 117
Tridents were built.
British Airways (two); BAe

147

To achieve adequate control in the
rolling plane at low speed, without the risk
of excessive control authority at high speed
and consequent risk of overload, the
ailerons were in pairs, only one section on
each side operated at cruising speed, both
pairs at low speed. Air brakes, which could
also augment aileron power, were fitted.

In September 1954 the USAF ordered 29
of the KC-135 tanker versions and the
airlines followed suit with orders for the
airliner, Pan Am being first in the field,
ordering 20 in October 1955.

Boeing's great rival, Douglas, also
produced an aircraft almost
indistinguishable in appearance from the
707. This was the DC-8. It first flew on
30 May 1958 and was a worthy competitor.
Its aerodynamic design was so good that it
became the first airliner to exceed the
speed of sound. On 21 August 1961 one flew
at Mach 1.012.

Yet another competitor in the same race
was the Convair 880 which first flew in late
1958, too late to make any impact upon the
airlines which were already committed to
the 707 or DC-8. A more powerful version,

the CV990 Coronado was first flown in 1961
and proved to have a performance
seriously below specification. Various
aerodynamic solutions were sought,
ultimately success was achieved, but it was
too late to avoid the record loss, by
Convair, of over $45,000,000 on the 880 and
990. It was a reminder that the price of
failure in aircraft design is a very high one.

De Havilland, in Britain, was desperately
trying to recover from the Comet disaster
and was building the Comet 4 to BOAC's
order for a trans-Atlantic airliner to
compete with the Boeing 707 threat — a
curious project as the much smaller Comet
had no such non-stop flight capability
without external tankage. BOAC was highly
embarrassed by the continuing delay in
operating the Bristol Britannia, a large
turbo-prop airliner intended for the
African and Eastern routes, later to be
upgraded to trans-Atlantic status with
increased fuel capacity. Bristol Proteus
propeller turbines were fitted and the first
flight took place on 16 August 1952. There
were many problems with the new engines.
The turbines flamed out in icing conditions
and on 4 February 1954 the second
prototype, flown by chief test pilot Bill
Pegg, with a group of KLM executives and
Dr A. E. Russell, the chief designer, on
board had a major engine fire over Wales. It
was uncontrollable and Pegg made a
masterly landing on the mud flats of the
Severn Estuary with no casualties, other
than the Britannia, which was a write-off.
Nevertheless, this fine machine went into
service but it was too late, like its
contemporary the Vickers Vanguard,
ordered by BEA as a replacement of the
Viscount. The concept of turboprop
airliners for medium and short range

149, 150
The Boeing Preliminary Design Group spent three years studying the implications of a new short range jet airliner even before the 707 flew. Acceleration to a high cruising speed in the shortest possible time was important on short stages, and the ability to operate safely from existing runways was essential with systems designed to ensure minimum time on the ground for servicing. It was decided that, as far as possible, components of the 707 would be used.

The wing became a crucial element in the design to give high efficiency at cruising speed and good low speed characteristics on the approach to short fields. It became one of the most advanced wings ever used on an aeroplane and resulted from many thousands of hours in the wind tunnel.

The result of all the studies was the Boeing 727. Powered by three Pratt & Whitney 14,500lb thrust turbines, the 727 flew for the first time on 9 February 1963 with 40 orders and 40 options on the books. United Airlines soon found that it was even cheaper to operate than their Caravelles. Since introduction into service, it has been stretched to carry up to 189 passengers at a cruising speed of 592mph. Range is up to 2,464 miles.

The 727 is unquestionably one of the finest airliners ever built. Once the unusual techniques of operation were mastered by pilots, its seamy reputation as a dangerous aircraft was quickly dispelled. It is probably one of the very few modern airliners to make a handsome profit for its builders, the total constructed would be around 2,000.

The photographs show: (**149**) a cargo version in Lufthansa colours and (**150**) the ingenious airstair offered as an optional fitment. It is electrically powered and may be extended or retracted in 40 seconds.
Lufthansa; Boeing

operations was completely outflanked on 27 May 1955 when the French nationalised Sud-Aviation organisation flew the Caravelle prototype for the first time.

This outstanding design introduced the now outmoded scheme of mounting the engines at the tail, a quite sensational innovation at the time, but one which offered the benefit of the wing being in airflow undisturbed by the passage of engines through it.

Passengers entered the cabin through a hydraulically powered tail-mounted ventral stair, which also formed a support for the rear fuselage during embarkation. The influence of the Comet was apparent in two respects. The complete nose section of the Comet 1 was used and the cabin windows were of a triangular shape, apex uppermost, with well rounded corners. They offered the passenger a reasonable view, reduced the overall area of the window and avoided the sharp stress inducing corners which had proved to be such a hazard in the de Havilland machine.

With its twin Rolls-Royce Avon engines the Caravelle was a particularly handsome aeroplane. An unusual feature for a jet aircraft of that period was the high aspect ratio wing with only 20° of sweepback — the Boeing 707 had 35°. In common with other turbine-powered machines, adequate supplies of hot air were available to overcome wing icing, that bane of piston-engined aircraft. The air was ducted through the area forward of the triple spar. The Comet had shown how the jet engine formula could permit a much shorter undercarriage with valuable savings in weight, the Caravelle, with its tail-mounted engines, went even further with a very small ground clearance. This, however,

required care on the part of the pilot when taking off, it was easy to drag the tail bumper along the runway when rotating to lift-off.

Development of the Caravelle was protracted, Air France operating their first machine on 6 May 1959.

This new short-haul jet proved to be economical over short stage lengths and completely confounded the critics who poured scorn on such use of a pure jet aircraft. It made such types as the Vickers Vanguard and Lockheed Electra obsolescent and proved to be the most

150

151
The BAC One-Eleven was a short/medium range airliner with a rear engine configuration and a high mounted tailplane. Designed to carry 79 passengers in a high density arrangement, it was later developed as the Super BAC One-Eleven shown in the photograph. The Series 500 Super had two 12,000lb thrust Rolls-Royce Spey engines and carried up to 109 passengers. Cruising speed was 540mph and the range was 1,420 miles. It has been one of Britain's best selling airliners — 230 had been built when production ceased in 1982. *BAC*

successful jet airliner developed by a single West European country. Some are still in service with charter companies.

The introduction of thirsty jet-propelled aeroplanes introduced another problem for their operators, major improvements had to be made in airport refuelling services.

The motor driven fuel tanker had been developed from the days of the 2gal can and chamois leather funnel technique, into a highly efficient and powerful machine capable of carrying over 4,000gal of fuel and pumping it into the aircraft tanks at a rate of 200gal a minute. But as aircraft continued to grow in size it became obvious that the tanker could not keep pace and using more of them was not the answer as airport congestion on the tarmac would reach dangerous levels.

The high speed of such aircraft as the Comet, Caravelle and Boeing 707 focused attention sharply upon the problem. Because of their speed, time spent on the ground was a higher proportion of their transit time than with slower machines, so ground delays were more serious. To compound the difficulty the fuel needs were much larger, the Comet for example, requiring two of the largest tankers to fill its tanks.

The hydrant system, now universal at large airports, was introduced in the early 1950s. Fuel tank 'farms' are located at the airport, from these tanks fuel is transferred by underground pipe lines to hydrants at the refuelling apron. Remotely controlled electric pumps are located at ground level near the tanks. A servicing vehicle is drawn up to the aircraft. This is connected by a hose line to the nearest hydrant. It contains

micronic filters, pressure regulators and meters and is equipped with hoses capable of refuelling aircraft from over or under wing tank valves. An important part of the system is the ability to make and break the connection with no spillage of fuel. This facility is built into the hose end which has a lever which opens the valve only when the connection is properly made, closure being automatic immediately disconnection is initiated.

The hydrant system has proved its ability to deliver fuel swiftly and safely and has made a substantial contribution to the reduction in turn-round time of passenger aircraft.

Russia entered the jet age in 1956 when the Tupolev Tu104 built for Aeroflot, made its inaugural flight on the Moscow-Omsk-Irkutsk route. Postwar development of civil aviation in Russia was rapid. In 1950 Aeroflot carried 1,600,000 passengers and 181,000 tons of mail and cargo, mainly in obsolescent piston-engined aircraft. The Tu104 was a remarkable stride forward, uneconomic though it was, with seats for only 48 people; technically it was primitive compared with its western contemporaries but it was good for Russian prestige, a more important matter than economics in the Soviet State.

The Tu104 was followed, in 1957, by the giant Tu114 four-engined airliner with turbine engines driving huge contra-rotating propellers. It cruised at 478mph, a very high figure for a propeller driven aeroplane.

From those two types came a series of jet aircraft through the 1960s to the present day, generally based upon contemporary

British or American designs, and contributing little to design innovation.

Two twin-engined short-haul aircraft made their maiden flights within a few months of each other in 1955. Of similar size and appearance, the Fokker F27 Friendship and the Handley Page HPR7 Herald were powered with Rolls-Royce Dart propeller turbines which had already been so successful in the Viscount. The Herald had begun its career as an intended Dakota replacement, with four Alvis Leonides Major engines of 800hp each. It soon became apparent that the Fokker design was superior, and that the Dart was a better engine. Indeed it was building a fine reputation with orders for the Viscount being placed by many airlines. The little known Alvis engine was not attractive to the market so the prototype was converted to two Darts. The first flight was made on 11 March 1958 by the chief test pilot, Sqn Ldr Hedley Hazelden. En route to the Farnborough Air Show in 1958 a major turbine failure caused an uncontrollable fire in the air. By superb airmanship Hazelden landed the Herald safely in a field with no injury to the nine occupants. The starboard engine had dropped off and only the rugged design of the aircraft prevented a catastrophe. This delayed development at a critical stage — Fokker had an agreement with Fairchild in the USA to build the Friendship under licence and Avro was working on its Dakota replacement, the model 748. This was a low wing monoplane with Dart engines and first flew as the Hawker Siddeley 748 on 24 June 1960.

One of the milestones in British aviation history was the notorious Duncan Sandys Defence White Paper of 1957. One of its main arguments was the preposterous hypothesis that in an age of nuclear warfare manned combat aircraft were an irrelevance and must be phased out. Many new and advanced projects in which Britain would have led the world in technology were scrapped. Most were military aircraft, including the Hawker 1083 Hunter replacement, the Saunders Roe 177 jet plus rocket interceptor fighter, the Fairey Delta fighter and the Avro 730 Mach 2 bomber project.

The civil aviation side of the industry lost the technical spin-off from these aircraft and was forced to abandon the new Vickers V1000 military jet transport, the first in the world to have trans-Atlantic non-stop capability. It was cancelled in November 1955, with its first flight only a few months away. The civil version of it, the VC7 could have been markedly superior to the Boeing 707 and the Douglas DC-8 which flew several years later.

BOAC bore some responsibility for this decision when, in an official submission to the Government, the Corporation stated that it was convinced that passengers would not wish to cross the Atlantic in a fast jet and that 'for the forseeable future it would be fully competitive on the North Atlantic with the Britannia. Shortly afterwards, in November 1956, BOAC sought Government permission to buy Boeing 707s! So Britain threw away its last chance, but one, to remain in the long haul big jet market. The last chance, the Vickers VC10, was also thrown away, largely by public denigration of this magnificent aircraft by the very airline which drew up the specification to which it was built — BOAC.

An interesting rotary wing aircraft appeared in the 1950s. After the war the Fairey Company decided to have a hard look at the helicopter market and attempt to eliminate some of the more dubious features of contemporary rotary wing practice. It was thought that the use of a tail rotor to counteract main rotor torque was wasteful and that a propeller acting in the orthodox manner on a fuselage outrigger on the side which counteracts torque would provide thrust as well as exercise its main function. So the Gyrodyne was built with a 520hp Alvis Leonides engine.

In 1953 one of the two prototypes was converted so that the rotor was driven by small fuel-burning pressure jet nozzles at the tips of the 60ft diameter twin blades. Propulsion was by two pusher propellers on the stub wings. After many development problems had been solved the machine was demonstrated at the 1955 Farnborough Show.

In 1951 BEA had issued a specification for a short/medium haul 'BEAline Bus' and a submission was made by Fairey for a large Napier Eland propeller turbine aircraft based upon the Gyrodyne. The airline showed interest and a prototype was built. There were so many unpredictable aspects of this unique design that an intensive programme of rig testing was carried out. A problem which

152
The handsome Vickers VC10, carrying up to 151 passengers, went into service with BOAC in April 1964 to the acclamation of passengers and crews. The Super VC10, stretched to carry 187 passengers, followed in April 1965. The Super had four Rolls-Royce Conway turbo fan engines of 22,500lb thrust each. It flew at a cruising speed of 581mph and had a range of 4,720 miles. 32 Standard VC10s and 22 Supers were built; a number are still in service with the RAF as VIP transports and others have been converted to the in-flight refuelling role. *Vickers*

153
The spectacular and beautiful tail of the VC10 can be clearly seen in this photograph. Note the Fowler flaps partly extended. *Vickers*

required very careful handling was the transition from the powered rotor helicopter mode to the unpowered autogyro mode where the blades are rotated by their passage through the air, propulsion of the aircraft being derived from the two Eland driven propellers. On 10 April 1958, W. R. Gellatly and J. G. P. Morton carried out successful transitions and the test programme soon reached the stage where a

record speed of 190.9mph was achieved.

For demonstration purposes the prototype was painted in BEA colours and several overseas airlines showed interest. In February 1960, Westland Aircraft took over the helicopter interests of Fairey and work on the Rotodyne languished until, in 1962, the programme was cancelled, to the relief of many who had heard the appalling noise created by the tip jets.

153

Another BEA specification was issued in 1957, this was for a short-haul jet airliner. Bristol, Avro and de Havilland made submissions of similar designs — advanced tri-jets with highly swept wings and tails and cruising speeds around 600mph.

The American builders were concentrating upon the long haul 707 and DC-8 so Britain had a splendid opportunity to dominate the short haul market. De Havilland's design was favoured, but BEA decided that it was too large so must be scaled down. This meant delay in both airframe and engine development. Rolls-Royce was forced to abandon its 14,000lb thrust RB141 turbine in favour of a 9,800lb unit, the Spey.

By 1960, when de Havilland was taken over by Hawker Siddeley, BEA's 24 Tridents, as the type became known, were in production. It was a very advanced aeroplane with wings swept at 35°, complex double-slotted flaps at the trailing edge and Kruger flaps along the inboard leading edge. Noise had been recognised as a highly unsocial aspect of jet propulsion but no concerted international standards had been formulated. Rolls-Royce fitted noise suppressing nozzles to the Spey turbines, but throughout its life the Trident remained a noisy aircraft. Thrust reversers were also built into the rear of the turbines to give a powerful braking effect upon touch-down.

Trident was the first airliner in the world to achieve blind landings in normal passenger service. It was the culmination of the dedicated efforts of the Blind Landing Experimental Unit described earlier in this Chapter. Three hydraulic units for the powered controls were installed, each engine drove one of them.

The Smiths Industries Autoland system, which carried out the final flare-out before touch-down, was a triplicated installation to achieve a fail-safe situation in the event of malfunction of part of it.

No Trident prototype was built, the first of the BEA order being flown by chief test pilot John Cunningham on 9 January 1962. The Chairman of BEA commented, 'It is the very last word in sub-sonic jet transport and is specifically designed for our particular network.'

In those words was manifest one of the worst mistakes ever made by a British airline, a mistake which was compounded by Hawker Siddeley's acceptance of the edict that the original Trident design should be made smaller.

On 9 February 1963 the Boeing 727 made its first flight. This aircraft was the same size as the first Trident and looked very similar to the production model. The magnitude of the error is apparent from the fact that over 1,600 727s were built for service with about 140 airlines whilst only 117 Tridents of all marks were built for BEA, Cyprus Airlines and CAAC, the Chinese national airline. The author recalls a comment made to him over the lunch table by a director of BEA in 1967, 'We would like to have bought 727s'.

There is little doubt that, in this case, as in others which can be quoted, if the manufacturer had showed sufficient commercial courage to defy the airline and had the finance to go it alone, the dominance of Boeing on world air routes would not be so complete.

The introduction of these advanced tri-jets with tail planes mounted on top of the fin, introduced unusual problems of handling. The complex flaps and high lift devices required the pilot to make his landing approach with a much higher percentage of power than was customary in a piston-engined aeroplane. The drag in landing configuration was high, so a precise balance had to be achieved to approach the runway at the right rate of descent.

154

154
Layout of the flightdeck of an early VC10. *Vickers*

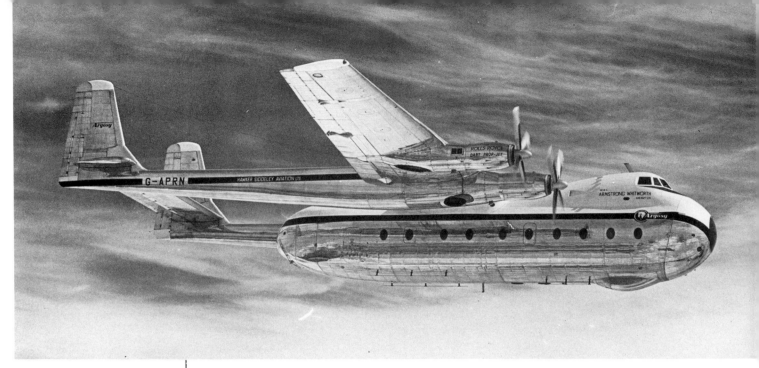

155
The Hawker Siddeley HS650
Argosy was powered by four
Rolls-Royce Dart propeller
turbines of 2,250ehp each. The
cargo hold was 47ft long and it
was possible to load a standard
9ft wide pallet into it without
difficulty. The flightdeck, being
above the hold, led one pilot to
comment that touch-down was
like trying to land a cottage
from the bedroom window!
　The Argosy could carry
31,000lb of cargo at a cruising
speed of 285mph. The range
was 2,100 miles. Seven civil
Argosies were built and 56
military transport versions
were built for the RAF.
Aeroplane Monthly

The crash of a United Airlines 727 at Salt
Lake City emphasised the nature of the
problem and the way in which the
searching enquiry which always follows
such an accident can improve safety
standards by what are often quite small
design changes.

On 11 November 1965 Flight 227, with a
crew of six and 85 passengers, was
approaching the airport in darkness; the
captain did not realise until too late that
his rate of descent was grossly excessive —
above 2,000ft/min when the rate should
have been 600-800ft/min. Full power was
applied too late to prevent the aircraft
hitting the ground 335ft from the runway
threshold, whereupon the port side
undercarriage broke away, followed by the
starboard unit. During the 2,800ft slide to a
standstill fire broke out in the fuselage,
caused by the undercarriage being hurled
into the underfloor section where it tore
away fuel lines and the main leads from an
electrical generator.

The accident was recorded as
'survivable', but 43 people died, most of
them succumbed to toxic fumes from
burning upholstery, which, even today, is a
serious hazard in airliner fires.

The outcome of this tragedy in terms of
aircraft design was a recommendation, by
the Federal Aviation Administration that
fuel lines should be re-routed to pass
through the floor beams near the centre line
of the aircraft, and that they should be
made of stainless steel thick enough to
sustain rather severe impact. It was also
recommended that the generator leads
should be re-routed to give maximum
separation between them and the fuel lines.
It was also considered that other aircraft of
similar configuration should be studied to

determine whether similar dangers existed.

A further serious problem arose with 'T'
tailed aeroplanes — the deep stall. If the
machine reaches a point where drag
increases rapidly due to a steep nose-up
attitude, the wing will finally stall with the
elevators probably locked in the up
position by aerodyamic forces. At the slow
forward speed inevitable in such a regime,
the airflow over the elevators is, in any
case, insufficient to achieve a nose drop
essential to recovery. The aircraft then
continues to descend with little forward
speed. Mike Lithgow, that fine Vickers chief
test pilot, with Dicky Rymer, late of BEA,
and their crew died in 1963 when a BAC
One-Eleven entered a deep stall. Under
identical circumstances, Peter Barlow and
George Errington of de Havilland were
killed, with their test crew, when a Trident
crashed near Norwich in 1966.

Various warning devices, such as 'stick
shakers' with a stick pusher are used to
warn the pilot and initiate action in the
event of an approach to this critical flight
regime.

Transport of freight by air was, by the
1950s, becoming an important aspect of
civil aviation. We have already seen how
the postwar Bristol Freighter proved to be
so successful in this role and, on 8 January
1959, Eric Franklin, chief test pilot of
Armstrong Whitworth, by then in the
Hawker Siddeley Group, flew for the first
time another A W Argosy, a very different
aeroplane from its venerable predecessor
of the 1920s. Designed from the outset as a
freighter, it was powered by four Dart
propeller turbines. To give easy access to
its capacious fuselage at front and rear, the
tail was mounted on two booms.

Used by a few airlines as a combined

passenger/freighter, and by BEA as a freighter, the Argosy was a commercial disappointment, the economic attraction of using obsolescent, and therefore cheap, airliners converted to freighters was much more desirable to operators.

In parallel with the development of the BAC One-Eleven, the Weybridge Group were test flying the new VC10 second generation four-engined long-haul aircraft. First flown by Jock Bryce and Brian Trubshaw on 29 June 1962, this very handsome airliner with four Rolls-Royce Conway turbines mounted on a beam at the tail went into service in April 1964 with BOAC, who had conceived the original specification.

The VC10 was received with marked enthusiasm by passengers because it was extremely quiet in the cabin. A high power to weight ratio gave a most spectacular short take-off and climb, but with noise levels which were appalling for those unfortunates living nearby. Structurally it was fairly orthodox; its superb handling qualities were achieved by smooth airflow over the wing unencumbered by engine mountings, with clever use of slats along the leading edge and Fowler flaps from aileron to aileron.

A stretched version, the Super VC10, flew in 1964 but damage was done to the sales prospects of the airliner when the new BOAC chairman, Sir Giles Guthrie, cancelled part of the BOAC order for Supers after widely publicised criticism from various people in the airline that it was not an economical airliner. Undoubtedly a weight penalty was incurred by the rear-mounted engines but it is certainly true to say that this innovation, designed to meet BOAC's specific need for good 'hot and

high' airport performance, created such a pleasant cabin environment that the type achieved a load factor, in its first year on the North Atlantic route, almost 20% higher than the average of 14 other operators on that route. The Super VC10 achieved 71.6%, other BOAC aircraft 60.8% and the other operators averaged 52.14%.

Overseas sales were handicapped by denigration by the national airline who were even reluctant to produce operating data to support the sales pitch. Charges of uneconomic operation could hardly be sustained in the light of figures of cost per revenue flying hour issued by BOAC in 1973. The Super VC10 cost £486 per hour compared with £510 for the Boeing 707 which was bought by the line. By that time,

156
The Pilatus Britten-Norman Islander in its latest form with Allison 250-B17C turbines rated at 320shp for take-off and maximum climb driving Hartzell constant speed three-bladed propellers. At 70% power, the machine will cruise at 161mph, the range being 500 miles. It is a tribute to the original design concept of the Islander that it has changed so little in the 22 years since the prototype flew.
Pilatus Britten-Norman

157
The interior of a commuter Islander. Well over 1,000 Islanders have been built.
Pilatus Britten-Norman

The Douglas DC-9 short/ medium range airliner was undoubtedly the company's most successful jet transport with a two-year lead over its competitors when the prototype flew on 25 February 1965. Initially seating a maximum of 90 passengers, the more economical BAC One-Eleven forced Douglas to stretch the DC-9 to carry up to 130 passengers.

The prototype, illustrated, had 24° of wing sweepback and double slotted flaps at the trailing edge. Double ailerons, the outer ones for slow speed control, the inner ones for high speed, were fitted. The 12,000lb Pratt and Whitney engines originally used have been superseded in the latest stretched versions by the much more efficient, and quieter, turbofans of 18,500lb thrust. Major structural and aerodynamic changes have also been made and the capacity has risen to 172 passengers in the Super 80 version. Indeed, no other airliner has been built in such a range of sizes.

At normal cruising speed of 515mph and with 137 passengers, the Super 80 has a range of up to 3,060 miles. Well over 1,000 DC-9s have been built for operation by more than 50 airlines.
McDonnell Douglas

of course, it was too late, and Britain lost its last chance to compete in the long haul subsonic market.

In 1964 the small Bembridge, Isle of Wight firm of Britten-Norman began work on a modern version of the DH Dragon Rapide. On 13 June 1965 the Islander was flown for the first time powered by two Rolls-Royce/Continental engines of 210hp each. Production models were fitted with 260hp Avco-Lycoming engines. In a cabin only 3ft 7in wide it accommodated nine passengers and the pilot. This had been achieved by eliminating a central aisle and fitting car-type doors for access to the seats. With its simple construction, fixed undercarriage and absence of complex systems, this low-cost feeder liner was an instant success and many were built for service all over the world. In 1970 market research had established that a 50% increase in capacity was required. This would need a third engine. The orthodox solution of one in the nose was out of the question as the ground clearance was insufficient. The designers achieved an ingenious solution by mounting the third engine at the top of the fin and rudder, the fuselage being lengthened forward to give the extra accommodation, and to balance the extra weight in the tail, which, together with the fin, had to be strengthened. The new design was called, appropriately, Trislander.

The end of the 1970s saw civil aircraft design consolidated into categories with a distinct similarity of appearance within those categories. Stressed-skin all-metal construction was predominant in all but the smallest machines. Pressurised cabins were essential as operating heights were

over 35,000ft — heights which achieved a very smooth and comfortable ride for the passengers.

Long haul aircraft such as the Boeing 707, its smaller contemporary, the 720, Donald Douglas's DC-8 and the two Convair types, 880 and 990, were very similar low wing monoplanes with about 35° of sweep on the wings, the engines being mounted in pods underneath. A divergence from the norm was the VC10, with its four rear engines, to be closely copied by the Russian Ilyushin bureau in the Il62.

These two aircraft followed the 'T' tail configuration, popular with a number of manufacturers, such as Douglas with the DC-9 twin — almost identical with the BAC One-Eleven; Fokker's Fellowship was also similar in layout to the BAC 111. The Boeing 727 and its Russian derivative, the Tupolev Tu154, were 'T'-tailed tri-jets, as was the Hawker Siddeley Trident, although the Mark 3B aircraft had an extra Rolls-Royce RB162 turbine of 5,250lb thrust mounted in the tail, below the rudder.

All later versions of Trident, and the VC10 fleet of BOAC, were certificated by the Air Registration Board for full Category III automatic landing in conditions of runway visual range of 295ft, and a landing decision height of 12ft, a remarkable achievement which was a great boost for the prestige of British manufacturers and airlines but one which has been slow to develop to the limit because of the high capital investment necessary in aircraft and at airports.

The medium and short stage airliners followed the Caravelle lead of having the engines at the rear, gaining the advantage

159
The Boeing 737 filled the gap in
the Boeing range between the
707 and 727 and met the
requirement for a short haul
twin turbofan aircraft.
Lufthansa signed the first
airline contract for 21 aircraft.
The first 737 was flown on
9 April 1967. It clearly showed
its origins by having a similar
fuselage to the 727, with the
same cross section as the 707,
an almost identical 707 tail unit
and a high degree of
commonality of components
and equipment. The under-
wing engine installation was a
breakaway from common
practice. The 737 has been
stretched to accommodate up to
149 passengers. This version,
the 737-300, has 20,000lb thrust
CFM International turbofan
engines. The 737-200 has a
cruising speed of 488mph.
Range, with 115 passengers is
2,913 miles. Well over 1,000 of
this popular aircraft are in
service with more than 30
world airlines.
This photograph shows a
Lufthansa 737-130 in the
landing configuration. The
leading edge slats and flaps are
extended. The double slotted
flaps may also be seen.
Lufthansa

of the wing operating in undisturbed air.
An exception to this principle was the
Boeing 737 twin jet with the engines
mounted closely below the wing but using
many components of the 727 and a similar
fin and rudder to the 707. The commonality
of components between the various Boeing
jet aircraft has been a major element in the
commercial success of this great company.
Stocks of spares form a massive capital
investment for an airline, servicing fixtures
are also very expensive, so it is good
commercial practice to continue to buy
aircraft from one manufacturer who
follows the principle of commonality.

Speeds of airliners were approaching
Mach 1.0 — cruising at around 0.8. This
avoided problems of kinetic heating due to
the passage of the machine through the air.
At supersonic speed the temperature rise
on the skin is such that special expensive
alloys are required, so cruising at Mach 0.8
is a reasonable compromise. Wing
efficiency is a vital component in the
economics of design, the thousands of
hours of wind tunnel testing had produced
a series of high speed sections which are
very thin — so thin that orthodox
constructional methods used in the
postwar types are outmoded. To obtain a
smooth contour, essential for aerodynamic
efficiency, riveted skin joints must be
avoided. Designers called for the upper and
lower skins to be made from a slab of light
alloy which would be located in a
computer-controlled milling machine. This
would be programmed to mill away up to
90% of the metal in the slab, leaving the
equivalent of stringers and other
reinforcing members as an integral part of
the structure and achieving maximum

strength with minimum weight and,
incidentally, eliminating many of the
sealing problems associated with fuel
storage in the wing.

The high take-off and landing speeds of
heavily loaded modern commercial
transports introduced serious problems of
braking on the runway. Thrust reversers, a
form of clam shell shroud which can be
moved across the turbine outlet to divert
the gas flow forwards, were a useful
contribution; tyres and brakes were
developed to withstand the enormous
levels of energy and heating created whilst
the Maxaret non-locking brake was a
valuable innovation. However hard the
brakes are applied, the system ensures that
the wheels can never lock with grave risk of
tyre blow-out.

The gas turbine had proved to be an
exceptionally reliable engine — a very
different machine to the original Whittle
type centrifugal flow turbine which was
hardly more complex than a vacuum
cleaner. The great Ernest Hives (later Lord
Hives) of Rolls-Royce, said to Frank
Whittle, as they looked at an early engine,
'Leave it to us, we will soon design the
simplicity out of it! These were truly
prophetic words when one studies the
giant RB211, generating over 50,000lb
thrust with digital electronic engine
control to schedule accurately fuel flow
over the whole operating range to achieve
fuel economy and savings in maintenance
through more precise control of operating
conditions.

The next stage in the design of civil
aircraft to establish techniques valid to the
end of the century includes the wide body
airliners and supersonic flight.

Higher Technology to Mach 2

160

The flaps of the BAe 146 being assembled. The broad section just under the trailing edge of the wing is normally housed right forward in the recess shown. To create high lift for landing at slow speeds the assembly moves out on tracks to give a deep curvature under the wing. The tabs at the extremity of the main flaps are then deflected almost vertically downwards. As soon as the aircraft is on the ground the lift spoilers, the three small panels just visible forward of the fixed section of the wing over the flap, are opened automatically to 'dump' lift and enable full braking power to be applied to the wheels. *BAe*

Several important developments during the postwar period enabled designers to exploit the power and efficiency of the increasingly complex gas turbine. The original centrifugal compressor had a frontal area larger than the more efficient axial flow turbine which soon became the norm. Power could be increased in an axial flow unit by increasing the number of compressor and turbine discs. With all gas turbines, noise was a serious problem and fuel consumption was high; fortunately they operated on kerosene, which was cheaper than petrol and had the advantage of a high flash point with, therefore, a greatly reduced fire risk.

The piston engine reached the limit of its development at 3-4,000hp. The Pratt and Whitney R4360 Wasp Major, fitted to the Boeing Stratocruiser, had 28 cylinders in four rows, developing 3,500hp. Magnificent engine though it was, its serviceability record was not good due to its complexity. The risk of engine failure on take-off with a heavily laden transport was a serious matter so the remarkable reliability of even the early gas turbines was an encouraging augury for the future.

The replacement of reciprocating heavy metal by carefully balanced bladed discs almost eliminated vibration which, itself, had far-reaching effects. As well as much improved passenger comfort, the life of instruments and electronic equipment was increased considerably whilst the absence of propellers eliminated another source of noise and vibration in the pure jet aircraft.

A major objective of designers was to increase fuel economy and reduce noise which had become a matter of public concern. A step in the right direction was the development of the turbofan which is a normal gas turbine used as a 'core' engine with extra turbine stages on a separate shaft running forward through the core engine shaft, or shafts, to drive a large diameter fan within the nose of the nacelle, this fan moves large volumes of air over the core engine to generate a high proportion of the thrust. The ratio of the flow volume of cold air from the fan divided by the volume of hot air from the core engine is known as the bypass ratio. This type of engine is making a major impact upon the economics and sound levels of high speed aircraft.

Powered controls had been developed to a high level of effectiveness and, with the great increase in wing loading of the modern jet, high lift devices were essential to achieve reasonable, one hesitates to say safe, landing speeds.

In 1930 the Handley Page HP42 had a wing loading of 9.4lb/sq ft, the 1937 de Havilland Albatross 27.4lb, the 1947 Airspeed Ambassador 43.8lb, the 1950 Lockheed Super Constellation had risen to 83.3lb; the DH Comet 1 of 1949 was a modest 57lb, whilst the 1954 Boeing 707 rose to the level, alarming for the period, of 98.6lb/sq ft. The Hawker Siddeley Trident, in 1962, was loaded to 84.7lb/sq ft.

A thin wing is essential for high speed flight but it does not generate high lift. The greater the degree of curvature on the upper surface, the higher the lift, so such a profile must be generated artificially in the take-off and landing phases of the flight. Several illustrations in this book show the

160

methods used. There are single or double
flaps at the trailing edges, usually arranged
to form a slot to ensure that the air flows
closely over the surfaces with no
turbulence. Variable camber flaps may be
fitted to the leading edges, either of the
Kruger pattern — hinged at the front to
swing downwards and forwards — or of
the slotted type, a modern version of the
Handley Page slot, sometimes a
combination of the two. These devices
produce a deeply cambered wing with good
control at low speed.

Spoilers or lift dumpers are other
weapons in the armoury of the aircraft
designer. These are hinged flaps on the
upper rear surface of the wing which open,
often automatically as the undercarriage
legs are compressed, to 'dump' the lift and

161
The tails of two DC-9-71s
showing the mounting of the
variable incidence tailplane at
maximum deflection. The
rudder trim tab may also be
seen. *SAS*

162
A Rolls-Royce RB211 engine in
a British Airways Boeing 747
undergoing routine
maintenance. The size of the
fan and the ease of access is
apparent. The RB211 has
proved to be an outstanding
engine, claimed to be, in its
latest form, the most fuel-
efficient in the world. It powers
Monarch Airlines Boeing 757s
and, in the first year of
operation, 3.3 million miles
were flown without an
unscheduled shutdown.
Rolls-Royce Ltd

163
A Boeing 747 in BOAC colours in the take-off configuration. The complex 18-wheel undercarriage was so designed to ensure that the giant machine could operate from normal runways without damage to the surface. The variable camber flaps will be seen along the leading edge. It will be seen that the location of the flightdeck high upon the nose permitted the passenger cabin, with its nine abreast seating, with two aisles, to be extended right forward.
British Airways

increase drag, thus assisting tyre adhesion and wheel braking capacity.

The 'all-flying' tailplane is another innovation which has become customary under the name of variable incidence tailplane. It is capable of incidence adjustment as a primary control function in pitch with elevators playing a subsidiary part as camber changing and trim devices.

Electronics in automatic flight control has eliminated the unreliability of thermionic valves which inhibited progress just after the war and one of its first triumphs was the automatic landing capability of Trident and VC10. The greatly increased operating height of jet aircraft introduced other difficult problems for the designers of cabin air conditioning equipment — a paradox which emerged in

the case of some of the first jets was the notion that the air louvres in the console over the passengers' heads were too noisy in the relatively quiet cabin!

The postwar emphasis on mass travel quickly dispelled the illusion that flying was only for the rich, and high density seating arrangements enabled charter airlines, in the 1960s, to offer two weeks in a Majorca hotel for £40.50.

The era of mass long-haul travel dawned in earnest when Boeing first flew their astonishing 747 on 9 February 1969. The outcome of five years of market research, the prototype was built in about 30 months from first cutting metal. Flight trials of this 317 ton monster designed to carry 385 passengers over a range of 5,677 miles were very satisfactory, although increased engine power was needed to compensate for increased weight. Certification by the Federal Aviation Administration was granted on 30 December 1969.

Pan Am began operations with 747s flying from New York to London on 21 January 1970. By July, one million passengers had been carried in the 747s. On 12 February 1971, equipped with a triple autopilot system, the type was approved for operation under Category IIIA conditions — with a runway visibility of only 700ft, or about three times the length of the aeroplane. This, in itself, is a tribute to the docility of the 747 which airline pilots have likened to 'flying a big Tiger Moth'! David P. Davies, who until his retirement was chief test pilot of the Air Registration Board, told the author that the two aircraft he most enjoyed flying were the 747 and Concorde.

By February 1984 10 variants of the 747 had been produced, some with the ability to carry 600 passengers or over 125 tons of cargo. Boeing claim a greater payload range, lower operating costs and higher passenger preference levels than all other wide-bodied airliners.

A supersonic airliner had, for years, attracted the attention of aircraft designers as the ultimate challenge. On 2 March 1969, André Turcat, chief test pilot of Aerospatiale, flew the French-built prototype of the BAC/Aerospatiale Concorde from Toulouse, to be followed on 9 April by the British-built Concorde, flown from Filton by Brian Trubshaw, chief test pilot of BAC.

Construction of this beautiful aeroplane, considered by many to be the most elegant ever built, began in 1965 after an intensive programme of market and technical research. Only a joint international effort could sustain the immense expense of such a project. Sud Aviation, as Aerospatiale was known in the early 1960s when the agreement was signed, was considering a supersonic development of their successful Caravelle, whilst, at Filton, the Bristol design office had an Olympus engined supersonic project, the Type 223.

Not until October 1947 had the American Capt Charles Yeager flown the Bell X1 rocket-propelled aircraft at Mach 1.015, only marginally in excess of the speed of sound, after being air-launched from beneath a B-29 bomber. Britain had abandoned its own chance of being first in the field in 1946, by scrapping the equally marginal Miles M52 design. In 1948 Wg Cdr Roland P. Beamont, chief test pilot of

English Electric, had flown an American XP-86 Sabre fighter at sonic speed and John Derry had also achieved Mach 1.0 in exceptionally dangerous circumstances flying the swept-wing tail-less DH108, an earlier version of which had killed Geoffrey de Havilland Jnr during an attempt at supersonic flight.

'Bee' Beamont had flown the English Electric P1A, the machine from which the Lightning was developed, at Mach 1.0 in August 1954 whilst Peter Twiss, Fairey's chief test pilot had set up a new world air speed record of 1,132mph in March 1956, flying the Fairey FD2, so Britain had some practical flying experience to add to thousands of hours of painstaking wind tunnel experiments.

A number of different wing shapes were investigated, finally the ogival delta was considered to be the most promising for the speeds of around Mach 2.0 envisaged for the new aircraft. By the end of the 1950s two important experimental aircraft were being built; Peter Twiss's FD2 was fitted with an ogival delta wing for research in the high speed regime whilst Handley Page was building the small HP115 with a heavily swept delta wing for research at the low speed end of the performance envelope. It was a remarkably valuable, low-cost research tool which investigated, amongst other factors, the ability of a delta wing to generate vortex lift.

Vortices can often be seen streaming from the wing tips of airliners landing and taking off, these are of small diameter and high velocity. Concorde's vortices are slow in rotation, large in diameter and very powerful. As speed is reduced on the **165**

164
Plenty of room for the duty free! 747 cabin interior showing the original sidewall stowage bins to the left of the picture and the later enlarged ones on the right. *Boeing*

165
A Lufthansa 747-230 cargo aircraft. The forward section of the fuselage is being loaded by means of a powered screw-lift platform. International standard containers and pallets move on rollers forming both the platform floor and the floor of the aircraft, whilst the equipment in the freight terminal is designed to ensure that loading and unloading is a very swift operation. The aircraft shown can carry up to 29 10ft containers on the main deck as well as additional container pallets below the floor — a total of 98 tons.

A Boeing 747-200C with four 54,750lb Pratt and Whitney JT9D turbofans has a cruising speed of 562mph, over a range of 5,109 miles with up to 550 passengers. Over 600 have been built. *Lufthansa*

166

166
Concorde taking off with the nose drooped to 5°. For landing it is lowered through the full travel of 12½°. Just below the flightdeck may be seen one of the small foreplanes, or 'moustaches', which smooth the air over the inner section of the wing where vortex lift is at its minimum. The small wheels under the tail prevent damage if the pilot should land or rotate at too steep an angle.
British Airways

167

167
Concorde flightdeck showing the complex array of instruments. *BAe*

nose of Concorde, like that of the BAC 221, as the FD2 became, is drooped to improve the pilot's view.

These two important research aircraft may now be seen at the Fleet Air Arm Museum at Yeovilton with one of the two Concorde prototypes.

A difficult technical problem faced by the Concorde design team was the shift of the centre of pressure aft when the aeroplane achieves Mach 1.0, a nose-down pitch being induced. Elevators cannot be used to overcome this as the drag penalty would be intolerable. It was decided to pump fuel from the forward tanks to one in the tail to regain trim. Between take-off and Mach 2.0 20 tons of fuel are moved to shift the centre of gravity 6ft; as the speed is reduced, the reverse procedure is followed. The fuel is also used as a 'heat sink' to dissipate some of the kinetic heating created by air friction generated at a speed faster than a rifle bullet.

In common with other functions the fuel transfer is computer-controlled; another vital computerised service is the actuation of the complex system of intake vanes and ramps in the engine nacelles to ensure that, at all stages of the flight, the air entrainment into the powerful Olympus

approach and the angle of attack increased, drag increases sharply without any tendency to induce a stall as the vortices move slowly from tip to root, covering the whole wing and increasing suction.
Because of the steep angle of attack, the

168

168
Dr A. E. Russell, now
Sir Archibald, who was head of
the UK Concorde design and
development team until his
retirement in 1971, with Brian
Trubshaw, Director, Flight Test
and Concorde, British
Aerospace. Sir Archibald has
just experienced supersonic
flight for the first time, a flight
which coincided with
notification of the Guggenheim
Award for 1971. This most
prestigious American award
was for his many contributions
to aircraft engineering and for
his outstanding leadership of
the UK team developing
Concorde. After experience in
the Bristol stress office in the
1920s he worked on such
important projects as the first
British metal stressed skin
aircraft which led to the
Blenheim bomber. In 1936 he
was made head of the Technical
Office, becoming Chief Designer
in 1943 and Technical Director
with responsibility for the
helicopter side, the Freighter
and the Britannia. He is a
Hon DSc of Bristol University,
was awarded the Royal
Aeronautical Society Gold
Medal in 1955, CBE in 1956, the
American Elmer A. Sperry
Award in 1983 for his work on
Concorde. In 1970 he was
elected Fellow of the Royal
Society and was knighted in
1971.
Brian Trubshaw was
nominated as British lead pilot
for the Concorde project in 1965
and was responsible for a test
programme involving eight
aircraft and 5,500 flying hours
from first flight to the beginning
of commercial services. He has
received many awards during
his test flying career and, in
1964 was awarded the OBE,
becoming, in 1970, a
Companion of that Order.
British Airways

engines is controlled to give the maximum efficiency and minimum fuel consumption, which, of course, is at its maximum when the after-burners are engaged for take-off and acceleration to Mach 2.0 with fuel being injected directly into the exhaust.

The flying controls consist only of a rudder and the elevons. The elevons function as combined elevators and ailerons, hence their name. To control pitch they operate in unison, in the roll mode they are moved differentially. There are no landing flaps, the wing of Concorde is of a subtle shape developed from many hours of wind tunnel testing, it has a combined twist and droop. The control surfaces are powered hydraulically, the actuators themselves being signalled by electrical impulses generated by the movement of rudder pedals and control column. This technique, known as 'fly by wire', is of immense significance in the development of modern aeroplanes. The 'wire' element is likely to be replaced by light signals passing along fine fibre optic filaments. This will save considerable weight by eliminating miles of copper wire.

The unprecedented complexity of the Concorde project caused an alarming escalation of costs in addition to the

runaway increase in the price of fuel which occurred. It became a 'political' aeroplane, castigated by powerful interests within the Government and outside it. *The Economist* with true Luddite fervour, condemned it out of hand, there was even an Anti-Concorde Project run by a vociferous gentleman whose bearded visage was to be seen frequently in television programmes. Even BOAC expressed a measure of disinterest.

Fortunately, the steadfastness of its supporters routed the Jeremiahs and, in spite of all the problems of the sonic boom, inseparable from supersonic flight, and high fuel costs, quite unpredictable when design commenced, the Concorde survived to enter service with British Airways and Air France simultaneously on 21 January 1976 proving to be as efficient as it is beautiful, with a splendid safety and reliability record unmatched by many of its subsonic predecessors. On the London-New York services it has achieved very high load factors on the 3½hr flight between the two capital cities.

A measure of the profitability of the aircraft is the fact that *Alpha Golf*, G-BOAG, after a two-year period of inactivity, other than being stripped for

169
A McDonnell Douglas DC-10 in the new SAS livery. Powered by 52,000lb thrust GE CF6, or 53,000lb Pratt and Whitney JT9D turbofans, the type can carry up to 380 passengers at a cruising speed of 594mph with a range of 4,606 miles. Over 350 were built. *SAS*

170
Interior of the DC-10.

spares since 1982, has been brought into service again as British Airways' seventh Concorde and it is even rumoured that the line may purchase some of the Air France machines.

Alpha Golf has flown 1,400hrs — the Concorde with the highest number of hours in its log book has flown over 8,500hrs in 2,300 supersonic flights. In March 1985 the static test programme was terminated after the specimen airframe had completed the equivalent of 20,000 supersonic flights. Very little trouble has been experienced and it is considered that it will be another 16 years before a passenger carrying Concorde will exceed the equivalent flying time.

It is a tribute to the talent of British and French engineers on the airframe and engine projects that such a difficult and complex international venture can be brought to such a triumphant conclusion, although Sir Archibald Russell, one of the senior designers, once said to the author 'I

don't know what all the fuss is about, it is only a paper dart, and they always fly!'

Knowledge that Boeing were working on a giant airliner led Douglas and Lockheed to follow suit to meet an American Airlines requirement for their domestic routes.

Both companies decided upon a tri-jet layout with a wide-body configuration, capable of being stretched for long-haul operation. The choice of engine would be left to the purchaser.

Very similar in appearance, the two prototypes flew within a few months of each other in 1970 — the DC-10 on 29 August, the Lockheed L1011 Tristar on 17 November.

Against stiff competition, and aided by the current favourable rate of exchange, Rolls-Royce won the contract for the Tristar engines, at a fixed price, delivery to commence in September 1971, 4½ years later, with a certificated thrust of 42,000lb.

This 'paper' engine was of a size and complexity which was well outside the experience of this famous engine builder. Their American rivals General Electric and Pratt & Whitney were already developing basic engines for the 747 which could be up-rated for the two new machines.

Rolls-Royce decided that weight could be saved by using a new and very strong composite material, carbon fibre, for the blades of the great 7ft dia fan of the projected RB211 engine. The carbon fibre fan was a failure and the engine trials on the test beds were extremely disappointing, power being well down on the predicted performance. The story of the disastrous early years of the RB211 is well told in Sir Stanley Hooker's book *Not Much*

Of An Engineer; suffice to say, in this narrative, that it bankrupted Rolls-Royce and almost ruined Lockheed.

Nevertheless, it was developed into an outstanding engine, which has powered more Boeing 747s than either Pratt and Whitney or General Electric engines and has been described by Colonel Borman, President and Chief Executive of Eastern Airlines, as the 'finest airline engine in the world'.

The DC-10 and the Tristar went into airline service in August 1971 and April 1972, respectively, and are liked by passengers, in spite of the well publicised accidents to the DC-10 in the 1970s. One of these, near Paris in March 1974, shows yet again how a simple design failure can have catastrophic consequences.

A cargo door at the rear of the Turkish Airlines machine appeared to be locked as it left the ramp at Orly Airport. At 11,500ft the 48in by 44in door, which sealed a compartment below the cabin floor, blew out, causing the differential pressure of 4.5lb/sq in to be applied to the floor which was not designed to withstand such a load. It distorted downwards and broke up in places, jamming the control runs underneath. The captain was helpless to avoid a dive to the ground which killed 346 people.

The DC-10 and TriStar are still giving good service on the air routes of the world; the slump in the air travel market during the 1970s ensured that neither aircraft reached its break-even figure of sales. Lockheed has ceased production of the TriStar after announcing a $2.5billion write-off on the machine which many in the

industry consider to be a fine one, ahead of its time.

The DC-10 is still in limited production as an airliner with the USAF taking a number of them in the KC-10 tanker version.

The early 1960s led manufacturers to the conclusion that the only possible chance for European firms to compete with the Americans lay in co-operative multi-national projects. Moderately successful as the Caravelle and BAC One-Eleven were, they proved beyond doubt that much larger resources were needed with a consistent long term development policy.

The market for short/medium range, ie, up to about 2,000 miles, was considered to be about 70% of the whole airliner market so most of the European companies were studying designs for it. Sud Aviation, in

171
All A310-300s will have the new drag-reducing wing tip fences.
Airbus Industrie

172
The second generation Airbus A300-600, derived from the A310. This Kuwait Airlines machine shows the flaps in the take-off position, moved slightly aft and downwards to obtain extra lift. In the landing phase, they move to the rear of the curved tracks and are sharply inclined downwards whilst the leading edge slats are moved forward to create a slot between their inner surfaces and the upper nose surface of the wing.
Airbus Industrie

173
Airbus A310 First Class cabin.
Swissair

174
The flightdeck common to the A310 and the A300-600. Designed for two-pilot operation, all instruments needed for the management of the flight are on the front, or overhead, panels. Push-button controls have largely replaced conventional levers. Systems are automatically monitored and all information presented on the instruments is based upon the 'need to know' principle, related to the particular moment. Malfunction warnings flash in colour on the appropriate system push-button. White signifies that the service has been switched off, yellow ochre warns the pilot that he may have to intervene whilst the traditional red alarm demands instant corrective action.

Six small cathode ray tubes replace conventional instruments. Two of them, in front of each pilot, give the navigation and primary flight display information whilst the two on the centre console, known as the Electronic Control Centralised Aircraft Monitoring System display, ECAM, provide information, visible to both pilots, on the technical status of the aircraft enabling them to monitor failures or potential failures.

On the left-hand CRT the messages concerning the failure, as well as the action required, are written in clear language, the originating failure being treated first.

The right-hand CRT displays the system related to a particular phase of the flight. In case of a failure the faulty system shows up immediately. During the flight the pilots can instantly call up a report on any of the systems. The ECAM display system is, so far, unique to Airbus aircraft.

The Primary Flight Display, the upper CRT in front of the pilots, replaces the traditional artificial horizon with a computer generated electronic image. The air speed indicator is replaced by a speed scale upon which is superimposed a yellow circle with an arrow which indicates the air speed. At constant speed the arrow disappears, if speed decreases, the arrow points downwards. Other speeds, such as V1 (take-off decision speed) or V2 (take-off safety speed) and the speed at which flaps should be raised, are calculated by the computer according to the take-off weight of the aeroplane and are presented on the screen.

The lower CRT concentrates upon navigation, showing aircraft position in relation to way-points, radio beacons and airports on the selected flight plan and may also be used to identify areas of turbulence.

The flight plan is programmed into the computer of the Flight Management System and, through the Inertial Guidance System, the precise position of the aircraft can be displayed at any time on one of the CRTs in front of the pilots who can up-date the computer information at any time, if, for example, air traffic control instructions or latest weather forecasts make a change necessary.

Information shown on the two CRTs in front of the pilots can be switched from one instrument to the other if required, a facility also available in the ECAM system. Course and height are controlled automatically and engine thrust is continually monitored and adjusted to achieve optimum fuel efficiency. At any time the captain may override the system. *Airbus Industrie*

175
The next stage in Airbus flightdeck development is shown in the artist's impression of the Airbus A320 where the conventional control columns have been replaced by short levers on the side console. The remarkable facilities available to pilots of this range of airliners are made possible by the use of electrically signalled 'fly-by-wire' controls. The A310 has the world's first 'intelligent' avionics system, built by GEC Avionics, to control and monitor the position of the powerful slats and flaps in relation to commands from the flight deck. It prevents premature retraction of slats and flaps through dis-similar microprocessors which are independently programmed to ensure a 'fail-safe' operation. It will detect electronic, electro-hydraulic or mechanical failure which could lead to runaway controls, and conveys the information to the pilots. *Airbus Industrie*

176
Airbus wings being built at the British Aerospace works near Chester. The massive assembly jigs may be seen in the background. *BAe*

A 320 Cockpit
Artist view

France, and a joint company formed by the German industry, called Deutsche Airbus, agreed to collaborate in the design of an airframe — the British Government showed no interest so Hawker Siddeley Group took a private stake in the project, by designing the wings, to be built at their Hawarden, Chester factory.

America had not entered the twin engine, twin aisle, short-range market in 1969 so the new consortium had a head start with a design to carry 250 passengers. The clumsy name Airbus was coined with the object of appearing to bring air travel out of the luxury market. The machine was to be known as the Airbus Industrie A300.

The prototype flew on 28 October 1972, followed by three more aircraft. French and German certification was awarded in March 1974 followed by American FAA certification, including automatic approach and landing in Category 2 weather conditions, decision height, 200-100ft and runway visual range, 2,600 to 1,300ft.

Rolls-Royce had been so deeply involved in the development problems of the RB211 engine for the TriStar that they were unable to work on the RB207, envisaged at one stage as the power unit for an early 300 passenger Airbus design. So General Electric CF50 advanced technology turbofans of 52,500lb thrust were installed in the A300B.

Air France and Lufthansa were enthusiastic supporters of the project and the first Air France Airbus went into service on 23 May 1974 on the Paris-London route.

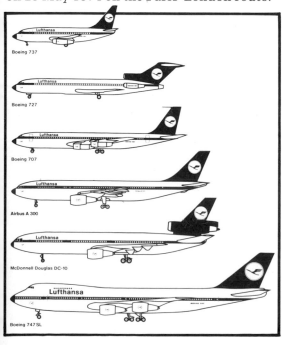

Passengers were impressed with it, as were people living near to airports because it was substantially quieter than most jet transports.

Orders were alarmingly few, only one machine being sold in 1976. By the end of 1977, however, 54 firm orders and 41 options were on the books and Eastern Airlines, the US carrier, was evaluating four of them which formed the basis of a 32 aircraft purchase in April 1978. This was the turning point.

The advanced technology of the Airbus begins with the computer-aided design procedure which saves time in evaluating alternative solutions of a particular problem and can even show a perspective illustration of a component on a visual display unit, it can be used to compare the relative positions of fuel, hydraulic and electrical service runs to avoid problems of too close proximity. There is no doubt whatever that CAD, as the system is known, has revolutionised engineering and architectural design where the project is large enough to justify its use.

One of the competitive strengths of the Airbus is its ability to carry larger volumes of freight than its close competitor, the Boeing 767 which, of course, appeared later. Particularly attractive to freight operators is the facility of stowing standard LS3 containers two abreast.

The latest Airbus, A300-600C, which went into service with Saudia in April 1984, can carry up to 267 passengers and 22 standard containers in the freight hold. the convertible version has a 141in by 101in cargo door and, in its all-cargo configuration, can carry up to 45 tons of freight.

The cabin offers true wide-body six abreast first class comfort, an essential feature for long haul travel. A wide variety of seven abreast business and eight abreast economy class options is also available to operators.

In April 1983 the new A310 version went into service with Lufthansa and Swissair, powered by two GE CF6-80 or Pratt & Whitney JT9D-7R4 engines of 48-50,000lb thrust. The A310 can carry up to 380 passengers in a shorter fuselage and it exploits modern technology to the limit.

A new high efficiency wing was designed, the section is a complete departure from conventional aerofoils with more curvature on the lower surface than the upper.

177
The six aircraft types in the Lufthansa fleet shown to scale.
Lufthansa

178
This photograph of the prototype Boeing 757 formating with the Boeing 767 prototype reveals their similarity in appearance. The wing span and length are, repectively, of the 757 — 124ft 6in and 155ft 3in — and of the 767, 156ft 1in and 159ft 2in. The 767 is powered by two Pratt and Whitney or General Electric turbofans of between 48 and 50,000lb thrust, each, and has a fuselage 4ft wider than the Boeing 727, carrying up to 290 passengers. Cruising speed is 528mph and the range is over 7,500 miles in long range cruise power with 211 passengers. The model 300, under development, will carry 330 passengers and will have a maximum range of 5,900 miles.

The Boeing 757 is powered by either the Rolls-Royce RB211-535 turbofan of 37,400lb or 40,100lb thrust, or variants of the General Electric or Pratt and Whitney turbofans of similar power. The RB211-535E4-powered version carries up to 239 passengers at 528mph. The range is 3,660 miles. *Boeing*

179
The interior view is of the United Airlines 767 mock-up, seating 197 passengers in seven abreast, twin-aisle configuration.

179

Such structures as the rudder, flaps, air brakes, undercarriage doors, engine cowlings and cabin floors are made of lightweight composite materials such as Kevlar or carbon fibre-reinforced plastic. This has reduced weight by just under one ton, with consequent benefit to fuel consumption. Even the auxiliary power plant in the tail has been made lighter and quieter.

Two man crewing is standard on the A300-600 and the A310 whilst all instrumentation and controls employ the latest push-button and digital techniques with cathode ray tube electronic displays for flight and navigation information.

The flying characteristics of the Airbus are superb, particularly at low speed, and it is one of very few airliners with an entirely 'clean' wing without such 'aerodynamic crutches' (as Lufthansa put it) as boundary layer fences or vortex generators.

At the 1985 Paris Air Show, however, the latest version of the 310 was shown with an ingenious design of wingtip fence which, it is claimed, reduces cruise drag by up to 2%. It reduces and controls the airflow from the high to low pressure areas at the tip and reduces the drag producing tip vortices. The swept delta profile avoids shock waves forming on the fence at cruising speed.

The ultimate accolade for the Airbus was the large order from Pan American.

In 1978 Boeing announced two new airliners: the 757, a short range aircraft to carry up to 196 passengers, and the 767, to carry up to 289 passengers over short or medium distances. The 757 was to have two Rolls-Royce RB211-535C engines and the 767 either Pratt and Whitney JT9D or GE CF6 engines. The escalating cost of fuel ensured that the lowest possible consumption was a vital necessity as, indeed, it had been in the Airbus design considerations. The most sophisticated fuel management systems were installed in all three of the new airliners.

The 767 flew first on 26 September 1981,

followed by the 757 on 19 February 1982. The Boeing reputation naturally generated great interest on the part of airlines, but it remains to be seen whether the decision to retain, in the 757, the narrow body section of the 727 was the right one. The diameter of the 767 is midway between that of the 727 and the 747.

Both aircraft are high technology designs, using composite materials in many components. The operating cost per mile of the 767 is claimed to be about 32% of that of the DC-10 and the TriStar so its commercial future is assured. The seven abreast seating, with two aisles, and only three seats in the middle, is bound to be attractive to passengers.

A striking new airliner from the British aircraft industry is the British Aerospace BAe146. This aircraft had been in limbo, as a design, for several years due to the serious slump in the air travel market. Ultimately the decision was made to go ahead and the prototype made its first flight on 3 September 1981.

The 146 is known as a regional airliner, a wider function than a feeder liner. It has some competitive similarities with the Fokker F28 as a short haul aircraft, but there the comparison ceases to be valid.

The design specification called for an exceptional ability to operate from short and, perhaps, ill-equipped fields, and to set new standards of low noise levels from the engines. In every respect the BAe146 has met these requirements with a handsome margin. With four Avco Lycoming ALF502 high by-pass ratio turbofans of 6,970lb thrust each, the 146-100 carries up to 93 passengers at a cruising speed of 490mph. The longer fuselage 146-200 will carry 100 passengers with a slightly lower airfield performance.

To achieve minimum maintenance costs the 146 was designed with the emphasis upon a simple structure with the minimum number of separate components. For example, the skins of the swept wings are made from a one-piece thickness tapered slab of light alloy. Redux bonding, which was pioneered 30 years ago by de Havilland, is used widely in the structure of the 146, it benefits fatigue life by eliminating stress raising fixing holes, gives a more even distribution of structural loads and helps to ensure a very long life for the airframe. The structural integrity programme which is in progress will terminate when the test airframes have successfully completed 180,000 flight

180

180
The flightdeck, common to both types, is spacious and uncluttered. The two central displays show engine information — the lower one, only when called up by the pilot. To left and right of the lower one are displays of the flight management computer system. *Boeing*

181
This view of the BAe146 taking off shows the ingenious design of the undercarriage, which, in spite of being retracted into the fuselage, has a track wide enough to give good ground stability. The flaps may also be seen, partially extended. *BAe*

182
The light and roomy flight deck of the BAe146 shows the pilots' instrument panel uncluttered with systems controls which are on the large roof panel. *BAe*

cycles, each representing a 45min flight.

The aerodynamic design of the 146 has also embraced the concept of simplicity, the wing section and sweep-back being selected for optimum efficiency on medium and short haul operations. A high wing layout was chosen because the continuous surface over the fuselage yields 4% more lift and 8% less drag than a comparable low wing. Fowler flaps, which add more than 30% to the wing chord, extend over 78% of the span to give low take-off and approach speeds. These benefits are achieved without the use of complex and expensive leading edge flaps or slots, and the wing design has enabled a fixed tailplane to be used with further advantages in weight and cost savings.

Multi-stop feeder line operations, especially in hot climates, impose a high work-load for the crew, so considerable thought has gone into the two-crew cockpit to ensure that pilot fatigue is at a low level. An auxiliary power unit in the tail will maintain comfortable cabin conditions during stops in hot climates. Comprehensive avionics, appropriate to the function of the aircraft, are installed with a digital autopilot and Thrust Modulation System (TMS).

In 1983 Dan-Air was the first British airline to operate the 146; Air Wisconsin was the first American line to do so, and both are well satisfied with the aircraft. Passenger reaction has been good although the high wing layout exposes passengers to a higher level of engine noise than a low wing machine. There have been some complaints of excessive cabin noise, but

considerable improvements have been made.

A visit to the Hatfield production line will confound the critics who could not believe that Britain has a future in airliner production. The type has proved to be extremely popular in the United States where noise levels at airports are taken very seriously indeed. John Wayne Airport, in Orange County is in a noise sensitive, wealthy residential area near Long Beach. In 1985 a rearrangement of operations to increase the number of daily departures from 41 to 55 was carried out. Strict adherence to a limit of 89.5 perceived decibels on take-off was demanded. Air Cal, with its new Boeing 737-300, the quietest of the breed, was restricted to an all-up weight of 100,000lb which enabled it to carry 100 passengers only as far as San Francisco, about 400 miles away. Pacific Southwest Airlines, with 20 BAe 146-20s on

183
BAe146s in production at
Hatfield. In the left foreground
the main wingboxes may be
seen. Study of the photograph
of the BAe146 flaps indicates
the relationship between the
fixed section of the structure
and the flaps. *BAe*

183

order, demonstrated, under the most
rigorous test conditions that the aircraft
was well within the limits at full load for a
flight to Kansas City, nearly 1,400 miles
away.

It is unquestionably the world's quietest
jet airliner.

The last airliner to be considered in this
chapter is also British. In 1963 Short
Brothers flew a small cargo aircraft called
the Skyvan, which had a strong similarity
to the Miles Aerovan of 1945 vintage.

The Skyvan, with two 390hp Continental
piston engines, was ultimately developed
with two 525eshp Astazou propeller
turbines. It used a high efficiency, high
aspect ratio wing developed by the French
firm Hurel-Dubois, in conjunction with
Miles, the rights of which were purchased
by Short Brothers in 1958. From the Skyvan
was developed the larger SD330 which
exploited new American regulations

permitting third level airliners to carry 30
passengers or a payload of 7,500lb. This
aircraft was originally powered by Garrett
turboprops, but later, Pratt & Whitney of
Canada 1,020eshp engines were fitted,
driving five-bladed propellers. Up to 30
passengers could be carried, cruising at
219mph over a range of 553 miles. A
retractable undercarriage replaced the
fixed one of the earlier aircraft.

The latest development in the range, the
Shorts 360, is powered by two Pratt &
Whitney of Canada PT6A-65R turboprop
engines developing 1,173eshp for
maximum continuous operation. This 36
passenger airliner, with the simplicity of a
light aircraft has shed its twin rudders, in
favour of a single one, and is as versatile in
transporting cargo as it is comfortable in
transporting passengers in the capacious
wide fuselage. The Shorts 360 is also
finding a ready market overseas.

8

What of the future

During the past 75 years the rate of development of civil aircraft has been as spectacular as the growth in traffic which was created by it in the decades to 1970 when fuel prices began to rise to levels which became a serious threat to airline economics.

The early airliners were small to meet the limited demand for this slightly alarming new form of travel. The primitive structures required limited design effort, limited tooling and, therefore, limited manufacturing capital; services were subsidised by governments in some cases, in others, operations on a shoestring were inevitable.

The introduction of the DC-1, -2 and -3, certainly the most significant basic airliner design, revealed a vehicle able to produce useful revenue without subsidy and maintain regular profitable commercial services almost regardless of weather conditions. All-weather operations required more complex navigation and radio equipment which, with much more expensive metal construction, required substantial investment in design and manufacture but the product could be built and sold in relatively large quantities.

From this date, increasing size, increasing speed and decreasing operating costs/passenger mile have continued to mark progress in commercial aviation.

Aircraft speeds have risen to around 600mph for subsonic jets whilst Concorde cruises at 1,354mph.

Payload/range capability enables non-stop flights to be made over ranges inconceivable, even with airships, in the 1930s, whilst passenger capacity has risen from four in 1919 to around 500 in the Boeing 747-300 with the possibility of stretching the design even further to carry 1,000 passengers.

Until 1985 safety had improved dramatically with the risk of a fatal accident to a modern airliner in the region of one per million hours flown.

The economics of the airliner for short haul work show little time is saved by comparison with rail or road travel. The short take-off or vertical take-off designs can be seen to offer possibilities of improvement if small airports near city centres are environmentally acceptable — one is planned for the London dock area.

Advanced military projects are, as ever, having a significant effect upon civil project planning but only a bold perhaps even foolhardy individual would risk prediction in this mercurial, and often dramatically innovative, industry.

The greatest stimulus possessed by that remarkable group of people in the design offices of the great aircraft, engine and avionics companies, and the research centres throughout the world is the combination of enthusiasm, an enquiring mind and the ability to say firmly that the word 'impossible' is not in their vocabulary — uneconomic, perhaps, but NEVER impossible.

There is a feeling in the industry that in past years new designs have been produced with greater alacrity than was necessary or desirable and that steady development of existing aircraft would have left the airline and the manufacturing industry in a healthier state. The success of the Douglas DC-9-90 and British Aerospace's development of the 748 into the new ATP model tends to support the view. The ATP is exceptionally efficient with low sound

184
One of the few aircraft using a ducted fan for propulsion, the Edgley Optica is a versatile, all-metal observation aeroplane following the great pioneering stream of Britain's aircraft industry — one man with a good idea and the determination to put his all into making it work. With a 260hp Lycoming engine, it can 'loiter' for 6½hr at 61mph. The fully glazed cabin is 5ft 6in wide and can accommodate three people. The Optica was designed by John Edgley himself. He built the prototype in his own workshop to a standard of finish comparable with that to be expected from a fully equipped aircraft factory.
Edgley Aircraft

184

levels achieved partly by six-bladed propellers.

Certain other trends emerge. The escalation of fuel cost has caused manufacturers and operators of aeroplanes to stress the crucial importance of fuel economy; the electronic engineer has allied himself with their cause by designing, as we have seen, clever fuel management systems to ensure the maximum engine efficiency throughout the flight envelope of the aeroplane.

The electronic engineer has also entered into the area of aircraft control. Conventionally aeroplanes are designed to be naturally stable, in other words, the centre of gravity or point of balance is in front of the centre of aerodynamic lift, and balance is achieved by the tailplane acting in a downwards direction. To compensate for this negative lift a greater degree of wing lift than the fuselage actually requires is built into the wing so more drag and weight is created, requiring more engine power and more fuel for the more powerful engines required.

A new system of Active Control is under development. In principle, the aeroplane is de-stabilised by moving the centre of gravity behind the centre of lift. The tailplane must then act in an upward direction to balance the wing, but, at the same time, providing lift, so relieving the wing of some of the load and permitting a reduction in wing area. The tailplane is now effectively acting in a positive sense and can be reduced in size by up to 35%; wing area is reduced by around 10%. Drag is therefore, lower and less powerful engines, burning less fuel, may be used.

Such a configuration would be impossible to control by orthodox 'pilot only' forces, but, with fly-by-wire and the introduction of sensitive motion sensors such as those used in the Inertial Guidance System, it is now possible to control the aeroplane through high speed computers feeding inputs to the controls and monitoring their positions many times a second.

Limiting parameters can be built into the system so that, for example, in the case of an aircraft flying through heavy turbulence, a violent up gust can be identified instantaneously and both ailerons deflected upwards to relieve the

185
The Space Shuttle *Enterprise* with its carrier Boeing 747 at Stansted Airport, en route to the Paris Air Show in 1984. The tractor and Houchin mobile ground power unit, under the nose of the 747, give a clear indication of the size of these two aircraft. *Houchin Ltd*

load on the wing; in the case of a down gust the ailerons would be deflected, in unison, downwards. Such a system ensures an even smoother flight in turbulent conditions, and it may well mean that the load factors built into the airframe may be lowered with a consequent reduction in weight and operating costs.

It is doubtful if major increases in speed will be made in this century, other than in very long-haul flying. As we know, 70% of airline flying is on short/medium haul routes, so, if we consider the maximum stage length of 2,000 miles flown by a passenger who lives 45min from his nearest airport, we see that so long as he has to suffer the irritation of arriving at the airport one hour before his flight leaves, substantial increases in aircraft speed will not be cost effective for him or for the airline.

With a runway to runway average speed of 500mph it will take him 6½hr to travel from his home to this destination airport, at an average speed of 308.7mph. A 40% increase in runway to runway speed, from 500mph to 700mph would reduce the overall time to 5.4hr. The overall average speed would increase to 370.4mph, an increase of only 20%.

This calculation underlines the problem of passenger processing at main airports with large numbers of aircraft arriving and departing.

A problem that is always paramount in aviation is safety, already at a high level. The electronic monitoring of every facet of every flight is likely to increase passenger confidence even further, although the dependence in crew training upon simulators raises the question of whether modern airline pilots are likely to be as effective in an emergency as their predecessors who were much more accustomed to emergencies in the air; what, for example, is the outcome of the unexpected, and *almost* impossible, total electrical failure in a modern, electronics dependent, jet airliner?

Interesting developments in propulsion are being discussed. The Edgley Optica uses the ducted fan which is quiet and economical, whilst the propeller may be revived for high speed aircraft. It was superseded when speeds rose towards Mach 0.8 as its efficiency at high tip speeds fell off dramatically. To achieve efficient airflow at high sub-sonic speeds wings were swept back, this technique is now being considered for multi-bladed propellers driven by gas turbines. Known as the un-ducted fan, or, irreverently, as a load of whirling bananas, it is likely to make a considerable impact upon aircraft design if it proves to be as efficient as its protagonists claim and test work carried out so far is extremely promising.

Early projects used a gearbox to drive two propellers rotating in opposite directions to increase thrust efficiency and counteract torque effects. General Electric of America found that the rotational speeds possible with swept back blades approached the speed at which a contra-

186
The Armstrong Whitworth AW52 was first flown by Sqn Ldr Eric Franklin in 1947 and was the culmination of years of research to achieve a true laminar flow wing by control of the boundary layer of air over the surfaces. Powered by two Rolls-Royce Nene engines of 5,000lb thrust each, and fitted with a special wing section designed to maintain laminar flow over 55% of the chord before turbulence occurred, it proved to have serious fore and aft instability problems and even dead flies on the wing surface reduced the effectiveness of the wing in achieving the critical laminar flow. It is conceivable that, with the new technique of active control the instability inherent in a tailless design could be overcome and the principle revived.
Flight via Aeroplane Monthly

rotating power turbine could be used efficiently and the expensive gearbox eliminated.

Sceptics considered that noise would be an insurmountable problem but extensive testing in an anechoic chamber by GE has demonstrated that the 25,000lb thrust UDF engine being developed for flight test in a Boeing 727 during the summer of 1986 will meet the Federal Aviation Regulations on noise levels and will be acceptable at that strictest of airports, John Wayne, in Orange County, California.

Wind tunnel tests have shown that it is efficient at low and high speeds. Noise, efficiency and mechanical integrity have been monitored up to speeds of Mach 0.83 and the goals for fan blade effficiency exceeded.

The UDF, designed for subsonic commercial and military transport aircraft is expected to offer fuel savings of 40-60% over current turbofan engines, or savings of 20-25% over equivalent technology future turbofans. It is likely to be used initially on 100-160 passenger aircraft. Boeing is designing a 150 seater to fly in 1992 with 22,000lb thrust GE36 UDF driving 12ft diameter fans. Rolls-Royce and Pratt & Whitney are known to be working upon similar engines.

Interest is also being shown in the canard, or 'tail first' configuration which lends itself to prop fan propulsion. Work has also been carried out on the 'slew wing' — instead of two wings swinging aft on two large and heavy bearings, the slew wing is pivoted on one bearing in the middle and swings in its entirety with one section swept forward and the other aft. It seems a rather improbable scheme.

The canard layout, with what is effectively the tailplane in front of the wing, is becoming a major development, possibly as important as the introduction of the monoplane itself. So far, it has not been used for a large aeroplane but the Beech Starship and Gates Learjet Avanti have continued Bert Rutan's pioneering work with very small aircraft. A possible difficulty with airliners may be that of compensating for centre of gravity variations in loading the machine. The Starship has a variable sweep foreplane whilst the Avanti foreplane is a trimming device, control in pitch being achieved by the third plane aft. Fitting flaps to a canard also introduces problems as large areas

can overpower the foreplane at low speeds. Reduced size flaps would necessitate a larger wing, so degrading one of the advantages of the canard layout.

For many years pusher propellers have been accepted as more efficient than tractors, the airflow from which is interrupted by wings, nacelles, fuselages and the tail planes. A pusher is particularly appropriate to a turboprop installation as the power is generated at the rear of the engine.

An American fighter design, the Grumman X-29, is under development with a swept forward wing which is said to improve manoeuvrability. This is not a particularly valuable parameter for a civil aeroplane but many advanced features of military machines have, later, appeared on transport aircraft.

Boeing is investigating a potentially valuable Mission Adaptive wing, the section of which can be changed at will and computer-controlled to achieve maximum efficiency throughout the flight envelope. Such a wing depends for its success upon the availability of flexible composite materials for the surfaces of the aerofoil.

New materials, many of them developed for the American space programme, have opened up new vistas for aeronautical engineers. Such alloys as aluminium-lithium, said to be up to 15% stronger than previous alloys, with less risk of corrosion and cracking, are an obvious choice for airliners where structural innovation is not likely to be rapid. The immense capital

187
One of the most interesting developments in composite structures is in the light aircraft field, exemplified here by the Robin ATL Bijou. Pierre Robin, the French designer, decided to take advantage of the slump in sales of American private aircraft and at the same time compete in a design competition held by the Fédération Nationale Aeronautique for a low cost trainer. His ATL design was accepted and an elegant aeroplane, likely to have as big an impact on the aviation scene as the 1932 de Havilland Moth, is receiving the plaudits of the experts. The ATL is of mixed composite and orthodox wooden construction. The fuselage is in two halves, split vertically, each comprising a moulded pair of shells in glass reinforced plastic, with a honeycomb core between the shells. The wing and butterfly tail are of orthodox wooden construction, covered with Dacron. The graceful cantilever undercarriage is also built of GRP. Engine options are a 65hp or a 75hp unit, both being derivative of the Volkswagen engine. With two occupants the 75hp ATL cruises at 122mph. Fully equipped it costs £22,700 compared with approximately £49,000 for its nearest competitor, the Cessna 152 which has a slightly higher performance, but with a fuel consumption of 5.2gal/hr compared with 1.88gal/hr claimed for the ATL.
André Baldet Aviation **187**

188
Unducted fan.

188

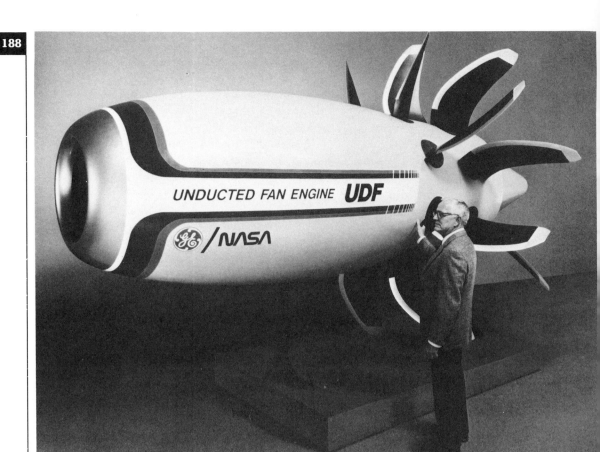

investment in orthodox production facilities and the long fatigue life demanded of modern transport aircraft ensure   that a long period of testing and proving of the new composite materials will be required before their use on a large scale can be envisaged. Nevertheless, composites, such as glass-reinforced plastic are widely used in lightly stressed parts and those where complex double curvatures would be costly to fabricate in metal.

Carbon filaments in an epoxy resin (CFC) form an exceptionally strong composite material which is being used for the rudders of the Airbus 300-600 and the Boeing 757 and 767, giving a structural weight reduction of over 15%.

Dupont's composite material, Kevlar, is easier to fabricate as it can be cured at normal room temperature, CFC requires high temperature curing in an autoclave. The whole of the gondola of the Airship Industries 500 and 600 airships uses Kevlar in the form of a one-piece moulded shell braced by all-bonded integral bulkheads and flooring in Fibrelam.

Computer-aided design techniques have enabled aerodynamicists to predict airflow over a wing in three dimensions and enabled highly efficient, or 'supercritical'

wings to be designed with sections quite unlike those with which we have become familiar. Such techniques have also moved into the turbine engine drawing offices where improved turbine blades have been designed and progress made in the development of ceramic blades which, due to their increased heat resistance, enable the complex air cooling ducts in metal blades to be reduced in number or eliminated entirely.

As we have seen in earlier chapters, fly-by-wire controls are commonplace. The next stage will be fly-by-light, the control inputs will be light signals passing through filaments of fibre-optic material in a lightweight harness. Considerable savings in weight will be achieved. It is likely that even more weight will be saved by replacement of hydraulic systems by small electric motors of high power, made possible by the development of very high flux density magnetic alloys such as samarium cobalt.

Ultimately all these savings in weight, complexity and — in the final analysis — cost, will achieve an even higher degree of aircraft reliability with a high degree of operating efficiency by computer monitoring and control of every aircraft function.

How to improve a plane.

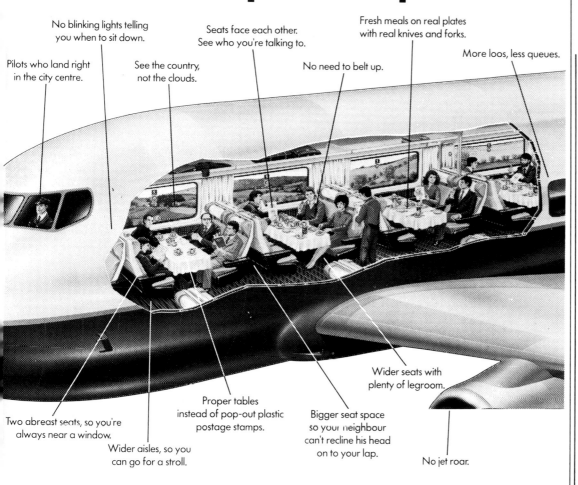

No blinking lights telling
you when to sit down.

Seats face each other.
See who you're talking to.

Fresh meals on real plates
with real knives and forks.

Pilots who land right
in the city centre.

See the country,
not the clouds.

No need to belt up.

More loos, less queues.

Two abreast seats, so you're
always near a window.

Wider aisles, so you
can go for a stroll.

Proper tables
instead of pop-out plastic
postage stamps.

Bigger seat space
so your neighbour
can't recline his head
on to your lap.

Wider seats with
plenty of legroom.

No jet roar.

We're getting there ⇌ InterCity

189

189
Many airline passengers will
agree wholeheartedly with
British Rail's proposals for
major design changes in
transport aircraft! *British Rail*

At the present time, supersonic flight is restricted to military aircraft and Concorde, which is really too small to be fully cost effective. There would appear to be a case for a larger aircraft carrying 200 passengers, but with engines of much lower fuel consumption and noise level than Concorde. A serious handicap is the sonic boom which, being a function of natural forces, appears to be impossible to overcome. It is conceivable that flight at altitudes higher than her operating level of 50,000ft would reduce noise on the ground.

The late Sir Barnes Wallis envisaged jet airliners flying at hypersonic speeds, over Mach 5.0. He made and flew models of his swing-wing design, the *Swallow*. Such an aircraft would be powered by ram-jets which must be accelerated to high speed before they will operate. Such a project could only be considered in the next century.

Another project which, a few years ago, would have been considered nearer to science fiction than science fact is space flight on a regular commercial basis. Although it can hardly be called a civil

aircraft, Rockwell International's Space Shuttle is already bringing space travel down to the commonplace. Launched for the first time from Kennedy Space Centre at Cape Canaveral, USA, in November 1982, the Shuttle parted company from its giant rocket to go into orbit, and ended up by making a faultless landing from gliding flight. As large as a BAC One-Eleven airliner, it has a payload capacity of 65,000lb and is now on offer to private industry for a fascinating range of advanced technology operations including repair of errant satellites and the construction of a space laboratory as a permanent facility.

It is a sobering thought, and a remarkable tribute to the ingenuity of man, that such achievements as have been recorded in this narrative have occurred within 80 years of the Wright brothers' first faltering excursions into the air. The advances likely to be seen in the next 80 years are beyond the comprehension of most men. Lucky, indeed, will be the chronicler of *Civil Aviation; A Design History* in the year 2065.

Appendices
1 Business Aircraft

190
A characteristic interior of a BAe125-800 showing four seats in an informal arrangement forward, the three seat settee to port and a single seat to starboard. The settee may be converted to a single berth. A toilet, luggage compartment and bar is standard equipment. The average passenger load carried by BAe125s is said to be less than three per flight. *BAe*

Postwar growth of business at an international level created a climate responsive to the suggestion that the time of a top business man was far too valuable to waste in travelling by airlines with the attendant delays at airports. Allied with this idea was the element of 'one-upmanship' inseparable from business and the proposition that the 'company image', that phenomenon which spawns a thousand extravagances, would benefit by the presence on the tarmac of world airports of the company aeroplane, even if some heretical shareholders consider it a conspicuously wasteful toy.

Be that as it may, business aircraft are with us in profusion and many of them are far more than the chairman's pet perk and fully justify their existence, particularly in a business with overseas ramifications requiring frequent interchange of personnel, or where, as in the United States, internal flying distances are substantial.

At the top end of the range is the highly prestigious 'biz-jet', virtually a small airliner with many of the technical features discussed in the last chapter and with a price tag running into millions of pounds.

First in the field was the de Havilland DH125, which made its first flight on 13 April 1962. A 6-8 seat aircraft with two 3,000lb thrust Bristol Siddeley Viper engines, it cruised at 485mph with a range of 2,000 miles. Its appearance was wholly functional, the elegant de Havilland line had gone for ever, but it proved to be an excellent design. The 13th production model was sold to the Atlantic Aviation Sales Company of Wilmington, Delaware, the first of many to be sold in the United States.

The DH125 was followed by the American Learjet 23 which first flew on 7 October 1963. It set high standards of performance and was a beautiful aeroplane, in direct contrast with the stubby DH125. Both types have been developed since those early days. The Series 2 BAe125 went into service with the

RAF as a navigation trainer, called the Dominie; the latest version, the Series 800, is in production at the British Aerospace Chester plant, 22 years after the first flight of the prototype.

Supported by the manufacturer's world wide service organisation, the 125 is still one of Britain's most successful exports.

The American Gates Learjet is a very elegant aeroplane, undoubtedly the most attractive business jet built anywhere in the world. The upturned wing tips are a striking feature of the Model 55, they control wing tip vortex flow and add a thrust component in so doing.

A highly innovative new design from Gates Learjet, as the company is now known, is the Avanti, developed in collaboration with the Italian Rinaldo Piaggio company. For the first time in aviation history, it utilises the three lifting surfaces concept. The main lift force is, of course, the main wing, control in pitch being achieved by the conventional tailplane on top of the fin. The third surface is the forward wing with fixed incidence and trim tabs at the trailing edges. This produces lift and enables the main wing to be reduced in size. It will be recalled from the reference to Active Control in the last chapter, that the ability of the tailplane to act upwards instead of downwards, due to the changed position of the centre of gravity, is advantageous as it allows the wing to be smaller, reducing weight and drag; precisely the same factors apply in the case of the GP180 which is powered by two Pratt and Whitney PT6A turbo props giving a high degree of fuel efficiency.

Beechcraft of Wichita, Kansas is another company following the canard principle in its new Starship. An 85% scale model of it was flown on 29 August 1983. Designed to seat 8-10 passengers, the production aircraft, will have a cruising speed of over 400mph powered by two 1,000shp Pratt and Whitney PT6A turboprops, the propellers operating in the pusher mode. The prototype flew on 15 February 1986.

The forward wing may be swung forward

190

or aft for trimming purposes, whilst the 'tipsails' are said to operate in the wingtip vortex area to reduce cruise drag. Directional control is achieved by small rudders at the trailing edges of the tipsails. As with the Learjet Avanti, composite materials are widely used in the structure of this extremely interesting aeroplane which owes much to the design ability and pioneering work of Bert Rutan, whose range of small, home-built light aircraft have followed the canard principle.

Beechcraft build all-metal aeroplanes from the single-engined Bonanza to the luxurious Super King Air, all direct descendants of the famous 'Staggerwing' biplane of the 1930s.

Rockwell, Grumman (now Aerospace Corporation), Cessna and Piper are four other American manufacturers of business aircraft. Rockwell has its twin jet Sabreliner, Grumman, the Gulfstream twin jet development of the earlier prop jet, now, the largest business jet on the market. Cessna and Piper concentrate upon a range of small aircraft such as the Piper Malibu, claimed to be the fastest single piston-engined business aeroplane with a top speed of 270mph. It is also said to be the world's first pressurised machine of its type.

The handsome Cheyenne IIIA has two 720shp Pratt and Whitney turboprops and has a cruising speed of 361mph and a range of 2,800 miles. Accommodation to a luxury level is tailored to suit individual requirements.

Cessna's Citation III is an impressive twin with Garrett TFE731 turbofan engines with thrust reversers. With eight

passengers it cruises at 534mph, has a range of 2,876 miles and can operate at heights up to 51,000ft.

In Europe, several manufacturers are in the biz-jet market: Marcel Dassault with the twin jet Mystère Falcon; Aerospatiale builds the twin Corvette; and Messerschmitt-Bölkow-Blohm, the HFB320 twin with its distinctive swept forward wing. In common with their British and American competitors, they have the engines mounted at the rear of the fuselage, resulting in a quiet cabin, except in the case of a BAe125 sold to a Middle Eastern customer with a passion for music. He had expensive quadrophonic hi-fi equipment installed which, the author was told by a pilot who flew the customer on a training flight, was played at full volume!

All of these sophisticated business jets are flown by two-man professional crews, the manufacturers having well equipped training schools to convert to the type.

Many business houses operate helicopters ranging from small three/four-seat machines to twin turbine luxury aircraft such as the Bell JetRanger or the Sikorsky S76 Mk II illustrated. It cruises at 167mph with a maximum of 12 passengers or 4-8 in the executive configuration. Helicopters are also used widely in the 'workhorse' role, as for example, in servicing North Sea oil rigs.

An interesting aspect of the total design concept inherent in the production and marketing of these business aircraft is the exceptionally high standard of promotional literature offered by the manufacturers. The Learjet and Cessna brochures are outstanding examples of graphic art.

191
The British Aerospace BAe125-800, the outcome of progressive improvements since the aircraft went into production in 1963. A number of aerodynamic changes have improved both performance and appearance, whilst the turbofan engines introduced on the Type 700 in 1976 have reduced fuel consumption and noise considerably. It has Garrett TFE 731 engines rated at 4,300lb of thrust each. The maximum cruising speed is 528mph and a maximum range of 3,400 miles. It can have similar electronic flight management and cockpit displays to the Airbus A310, described in the last chapter.

The sales performance of the BAe125 has been exceptional, over 600 have been delivered despite the world recession of 1982/83. Only the American Cessna Citation and the Learjet — both smaller — have sold in larger numbers. 60% of BAe125 sales have been to the American continent, whilst, in Europe, 115 are in service, making it the most popular business jet. *BAe*

192
The shape of things to come. The full size mock-up of the new canard type prop turbine Gates Piaggio Avanti executive/private owner aircraft.
Gates Learjet

193
On 7 October 1963 the prototype Learjet 23 made its first flight, 11 months after its strongest competitor the BAe125 (then the DH125). Its outstandingly elegant lines attracted attention wherever it landed and the type has been developed into the even more attractive Model 55, now known at the Gates Learjet 55.
Gates Learjet

194
The Learjet 55 is a larger aeroplane than its predecessor, with a cabin in which passengers can stand up. In spite of the increased diameter of the fuselage the lines have not suffered. With two Garrett AR TFE731 turbofans of 3,700lb thrust the Model 55 has a cruising speed of 523mph and a maximum range with four passengers of 2,767 miles. The cabin will seat up to eight passengers.   *Gates Learjet*

195

In 1932, Walter Beech left his design post at Curtiss-Wright to buy the Travelair plant at Wichita, Kansas and develop his own aircraft. From his board came one of the classic biplanes, the Model 17, affectionately known as the 'Staggerwing' from its back-staggered configuration which gave a good view for the pilot and excellent stalling characteristics. Powered by a range of engines from the 225hp Jacobs to a 710hp Wright it was in production until 1948, over 750 being built. Luxuriously appointed it was the fastest small passenger aircraft with a top speed of over 170mph, according to engine power. A few are still to be seen at air displays. *Aeroplane Monthly*

196, 197

The Beech Starship 1 prototype to 85% scale and its interior. *Beech*

198
Beechcraft Bonanza F33A.
Beech

199
The Piper Cheyenne IIIA. *Paul Bower via Piper Aircraft.*

200,201
The Sikorsky S76 Mk II and its interior. *Sikorsky*

2 Airports

We have seen how the rapid development of transport aircraft since the end of World War 2 has forced the pace of airport growth until the advent of the wide-body, long range airliner in the 1970s gave the planners a further problem.

At London's Heathrow airport passenger throughput in 1970 was 15,606,719 with 270,302 aircraft movements. A peak was reached in 1979 with 28,357,856 passengers and 299,030 movements. From this date the figures dropped to 26,740,811 and 273,068 respectively in 1982.

In the same period cargo and mail handling rose from 366,542 tons to 547,621 tons in 1979, this total fell to 489,377 tons in 1982.

In 1974 the average capacity of a British Airways aircraft was 95 seats, today the average is 160. It has been predicted that by the 1990s the average will have risen to 270. So the apparent effect that the reduction in movements by using larger aircraft will effectively relieve the pressure on airports is only valid on the 'airside' with fewer problems for the hard-pressed air traffic controllers. Unfortunately, development of airports is usually well behind the increase in passenger traffic which requires the expansion of facilities.

The question of airport noise is an exceptionally difficult one. It is a nuisance to all who live or work near to the take-off or landing paths of powerful aircraft. In Britain, millions of pounds have been spent on research by the Government, universities, research centres and the manufacturers to achieve noise levels which are more acceptable to residents in the neighbourhood. There has been international participation and, in 1986, international noise regulations came into force which effectively bar noisy airliners such as the Boeing 707, Hawker Siddeley Trident and the Vickers VC10 which do not conform with the standard established.

The jet engine is inherently noisy as its power depends upon a fast moving jet stream, which, itself, is a high intensity noise source. Palliatives such as corrugated nozzles have helped but the breakthrough came with the introduction of the fan jet, or by-pass, turbine, in which the high speed flow from the core engine exhaust is 'wrapped up' in the surrounding lower velocity flow from the fan.

This development also had a beneficial effect upon fuel consumption. The 160-seat VC10 was replaced on British Airways long haul routes by the 265-seat Tristar. The increase in aircraft size has not been accompanied by a proportionate increase in fuel costs and noise. The Tristar uses 43% less fuel per seat and creates only a fraction of the noise of a VC10.

Heathrow is the world's fifth busiest international airport and handles more than 23million international travellers a year — more than any other airport in the world. If domestic travellers are included in the total, it is fourth busiest, with 26.5million passengers in 1982. 45,000 persons are employed there and passengers of 74 airline companies fly to 215 international destinations on scheduled services. There are 125 parking stands of which 70 are large enough to take wide bodied aircraft. The cargo area has 12 stands, six for 747s, the others large enough for wide bodied aircraft.

An important function at any large airport is the provision of food for airline passengers. British Airways Catering Centre prepares 150,000 meals per week. The centre has kitchens, cold rooms, deep freezes, larders, and preparation rooms for fish, meat and vegetables and had its own bakery.

Such a vast output generates a formidable amount of washing up. This is carried out by seven large machines, fed by conveyors, to handle, in any one day, 90,000 pieces of cutlery, 20,000 trays, 50,000 tray dishes, 30,000 glasses and 40,000 cups and saucers.

The airline catering industry is pressing for a higher degree of standardisation in galley systems and there is a continuing battle between the advocates of

202

203

202
A tractor, ambulance, searchlight and Hucks starter on a Rolls-Royce Silver Ghost chassis at Croydon in October 1920.
London Borough of Sutton Libraries

203
His Majesty's Mail being loaded aboard HP42 *Heracles* at Croydon in 1931.
London Borough of Sutton Libraries

'disposables' and those of 'rotables'. Rotables is airline jargon for durable plastic or china crockery and metal cutlery. Happily, these are gaining ground although the losses are incredibly high — British Caledonian loses 40,000 pieces of cutlery a month whilst, at Stoke on Trent, two potters are hard at work replacing bone china sets 'absent without leave' from the affluent First Class, a remarkable illustration of the morals of the time.

The visual element in air-line catering is more important than the casual passenger might think. At altitude the high levels of ultra-violet light can made a dramatic change to the appearance of food; for example, a pistachio ice cream can change colour from a delicate green to the colour of green ink — not a pretty sight! It is a remarkable tribute to this industry that with millions of meals being loaded upon thousands of airliners thoughout the world

few problems arise for the passenger other than the inevitable appearance of a miniscule tray crammed with IATA specified comestibles. In the amount of room available in a high density airliner there is no alternative.

Refuelling of the aircraft is yet another vitally important operation, one which affects profitability of an airline. The system of tank farms and hydrant re-fuelling, universal at major airports, has already been described in an earlier chapter.

Passenger transit through Check-in, Immigration and Customs, with the associated baggage despatch and reclaim, is a time-consuming operation and an inevitable source of exasperation to travellers. The new Terminal Four, on the south side of Heathrow, is a trend-setter in passenger handling. Arriving and departing passengers are segregated on separate floors. Departure traffic is directed to an upper level forecourt to set down passengers, who remain on this level until they reach the appropriate loading bridge for their aircraft. Arriving passengers leave their loading bridge at mezzanine level and pass along the arrivals corridor to passport control. Passenger flow is improved and baggage trolleys may be taken right through the system which is of benefit to those confined to wheel chairs. Terminal Four caters for about 2,000 passengers an hour in each direction.

The building is yet another example of computer-aided design. In the boardroom of the consultant architects, Scott Brownrigg and Turner, of Guildford, is an elevation drawing of the terminal about 20ft long, drawn by the computer system. It is possible to superimpose layouts of all the services so that any locational interference between them may be identified.

The provision of power for starting aeroplane engines has been a requirement since the early days of aviation. When the power of engines increased to a point where the 'strong right arm' lacked the muscle to 'swing the prop', B. C. Hucks, himself a pilot of considerable talent, devised the Hucks starter. This was a horizontal shaft, adjustable for height, with a claw on the projecting end of it which engaged with an appropriate claw on the end of the propeller shaft or spinner The other end of the shaft was connected to the engine of the vehicle upon which it was mounted. An example of the Hucks Starter may be seen in the Shuttleworth Collection Museum at Old Warden.

The modern airliner may be fitted with a gas turbine auxiliary power unit in the tail to provide power for essential services on the ground. Environmental considerations of pollution are creating interest in Fixed Electric Power facilities in passenger loading areas and servicing hangars so that aircraft may be 'plugged in'. Desirable though this may be, the capital investment is very large, so for a number of years the highly efficient ground power unit will prevail. The loading of the systems aboard most aircraft is in the range 30-40kVA maximum whilst the cabin air conditioning and lighting, with galley services raise the power needs of large airliners to 90-140kVA at the standardised international frequency of 400Hz. The British firm of Houchin is among the leaders in this specialised field and builds a range of such units, some of which may be mounted upon the aircraft towing tractor, the smaller ones being merely trailers to be towed to the aircraft.

The development of air bridges, telescopic tunnels which can be extended and steered to align with aircraft doors, facilitate the use of Fixed Electric Power as the cables can be arranged to move to the aircraft with the bridge. The elimination of the bus ride to the airport is a valuable benefit to the passengers as well as achieving reduction in vehicle congestion around the loading ramp.

All these activities take place within the vital framework of air traffic control. Terminal Control Areas (TCAs) protect operations in busy airways and at groups of large airports in close proximity to each other. The airways connect the TCAs. These are corridors of space 10 miles wide from 5-7,000ft above the ground to a height of 24,500ft. UK airspace is controlled from two centres — London, based at West Drayton near Heathrow and Scottish, based at Prestwick, Ayrshire which also handles trans-Atlantic traffic.

The controller in the airport tower monitors on his radar screens all aircraft en route. These have a duty, when approaching the airport, to report their arrival over certain points. He will verify his identification of a particular aircraft and its height, by a call sign activated by a transponder through the on-board computer as soon as the interrogating signal is received from the airport radar.

Navigational aids, such as VHF Omni-Directional Range, Distance Measuring Equipment and non-directional beacons are available to pilots. Safe separation between aircraft in the zone is achieved and if traffic density is high, they are directed to a holding area and 'stacked' over a radio beacon where a vertical separation of at least 1,000ft is maintained.

In spite of the remarkable safety record of air transport, precautions must be taken in the event of accidents on the airport, or nearby. The most important vehicle is the fire appliance, the design of which has kept pace with the increasing size and fuel load of the modern airliner.

Gloster Saro, of Gloucester, descended from famous builders of fighter aircraft and flying boats, build vehicles ranging from the 90mph rapid intervention truck for fast transit to, for example, an engine fire, to the massive 577hp Javelin capable of pumping 1,100gal of foam per minute with a still air range of 65yd. It also has a telescopic aerial cage giving direct access to fires in high-mounted engines of aircraft such as the Tristar and the DC-10. The Javelin can travel at 70mph.

Snow clearance and runway sweeping are two other facilities which must be provided at airports while, to avoid the serious danger which may arise in the event of a bird strike on take-off, bird scarers are a necessary facility.

Heathrow airport and its organisation are characteristic of most of the world's large airports and it is probably true to say that a traveller arriving unexpectedly at any one of them would find the international style of architecture — good though it usually is — so stereotyped that he would be unable to recognise even the country. There are a few exceptions, of course. The remarkable architecture of the airports in Saudi Arabia and the United Arab Emirates are unique in their beauty and are architectural tours de force by any criteria. Others too, have distinctive characters — like Antigua, which presumably still has its welcoming steel band, and Honolulu with its reception committee of Hawaiian beauties wearing leis and bearing glasses of ice cold orange juice! A felicitous touch which helps to dispel jet lag!

204

204
Boarding *Horatius* in 1932. The covered way protects passengers from the propeller slipstream. *British Airways*

205
The cleaning brigade at work on a Junkers F13 of Lufthansa in the 1920s. *Lufthansa*

206
A Junkers F13 being refuelled at Croydon in 1927. *Lufthansa*

207, 208
John F. Kennedy Airport, New York, is the largest in the United States, covers 5,000 acres and handles 35% of the international passengers arriving in the country. (**207**) The terminal complex surrounded by runways. Concorde can be seen outside the BA Terminal at bottom right; (**208**) the control tower and Terminal apron. *Port Authority of New York and New Jersey.*

206

207

209
A leased DH16, inaugurating a mail flight from London to Amsterdam, landed at Schiphol, the Dutch Air Force base, on 17 May 1920. Located on a reclaimed polder, below sea level, the aerodrome was a muddy field 900yd square, giving a maximum take-off run of 1,100yd. Anthony Fokker built his aircraft works there and, in 1926, radio and night landing facilities were installed. Schiphol soon became one of the leading European airports and one of the first to have hard runways. By 1939 there were four of them. *KLM*

210
Schiphol Airport was utterly destroyed during the war and was soon rebuilt. Flying recommenced as early as July 1945. Since then, major developments have created one of the finest airports in the world where traditional Dutch hospitality abounds. The aerial photograph shows the new airport, Schiphol Central, the old one is known as Schiphol East. The circular building near the centre is the railway station. The dome shaped building, top right, is an aviation museum. There are four runways, 11,000ft long and 18 million passengers per year can be handled by the Terminal. *Schiphol BV*

211
The entry side and the air side of the Schiphol Terminal. The control tower is on top of the multi-storey office block. In the air side photograph the KLM A310 Airbus has just arrived, the forward air bridge is in position and the rear one is being manoeuvred towards the door. *Schiphol BV*

212
1923 view of Berlin Tempelhof. *Lufthansa*

212

213
Lufthansa shuttle buses
carrying passengers from the
airport to the city — Tempelhof
1928. *Lufthansa*

213

214
Passenger transport at
Birmingham Airport — the
world's first installation of
transit cars supported by
magnetic levitation is installed
to carry passengers from the
main line railway station to the
Terminal in 90sec. The
frictionless MAGLEV system is
computer controlled or
operated by passenger demand
to give a maximum waiting time
between cars of only two
minutes. *Birmingham
International Airport*

215
The diagram indicates the basic
principles of air traffic control
at a major airport.
Civil Aviation Authority

216
The United Kingdom airways
system.

214

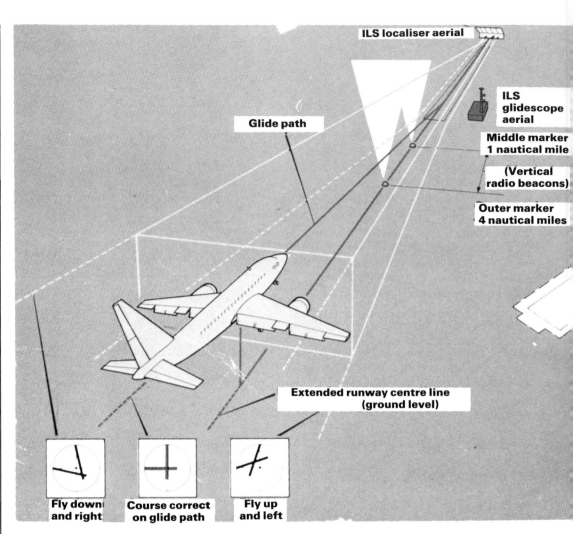

ILS localiser aerial

Glide path

ILS
glidescope
aerial

Middle marker
1 nautical mile

(Vertical
radio beacons)

Outer marker
4 nautical miles

Extended runway centre line
(ground level)

Fly down
and right

Course correct
on glide path

Fly up
and left

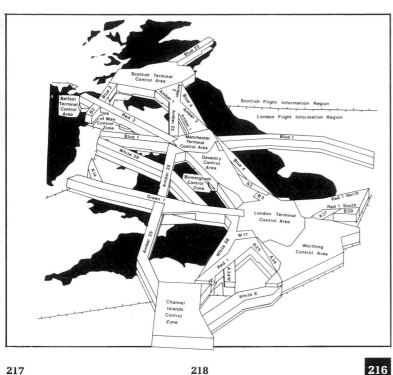

219

217
Alitalia's building at Rome Airport is called the 'City of the Skies'. This is the cargo building — note the simultaneous loading, through the nose and side hatch, of the Boeing 747 freighter. Hydraulically lifted roller platforms enable the operation to be carried out swiftly with the minimum of effort. Note the external load bearing trusses of the hangar in the background. *Alitalia*

218
A collection of airport vehicles at Gatwick. In the foreground, around the British Caledonian BAC One-Eleven with its airstair lowered, are an Esso refueller and a small tractor for towing the freight trolleys shown. The Dan Air BAe146 is approaching the airbridges, one of which is shown in more detail beyond the BAC One-Eleven. The bridge may be extended and elevated to engage the aircraft door at the right level. Driving one of these bridges is a highly skilled job and is licensed by the British Airports Authority. *BAe*

216

218

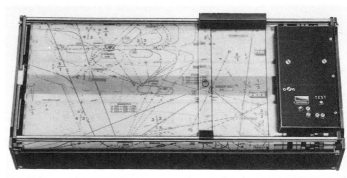

220

219
Navigational Systems
The first major development in electronic navigation aids for civil aircraft was the Decca Navigator. Prior to 1950, pilots flew along designated routes from beacon to beacon. The Decca system gave the pilot an accurate indication of the position of his aircraft on a flight deck pictorial display, permitting a course to be planned directly to his destination. The development of powerful airborne computers led to more complex equipment with far greater facilities for control and data presentation, from the Decca Omnitrac to the Ambac-Decca MONA System which collates, processes and displays navigational data from sensors such as Inertial Platforms, VHF omni-directional ranges air data and magnetic headings; the inputs passing to the automatic flight control system of the aircraft to give accurate horizontal and vertical navigational capacity. With Decca now in the Racal Group, the latest development is the RNS5000 multi sensor processing system. Space precludes a detailed description of this remarkable system which is said to be capable of amortising its capital cost through fuel/operating economies in eighteen months.

In addition to the general facilities of Omnitrac, it will accept information from systems planned for future use such as Global Positioning Systems (GPS) and Microwave Landing Systems (MLS). It will advise the pilot of the appropriate Mach No or indicated air speed to arrive at a given waypoint at a desired time and can be programmed to hold the aircraft in a given holding pattern in the event of landing delay. At airports the efficiency of such systems must be matched by those at the service of the Controllers. The Cossor Compass 9000 is one of them. 16 inch diameter high resolution and high speed cathode ray tubes present to the controller full data from primary and secondary surveillance radar, the latter being in the form of the aircraft call sign confirming the distant identification on the primary radar. The flight level is shown and the exact position of the machine within the range rings. Time, air pressure in millibars and the minimum stacking level for the aircraft are also displayed.

The photograph shows the installation at London (Gatwick) Airport. *Racal*

220
The Decca Navigator flight deck display. *Lasser Electronics*

221

221
Gloster Saro Javelin Fire
Vehicle with the aerial cage
erected at its maximum height
of 30ft.
British Airport Authority

222, 223
Major airlines have their own
simulators which are often
used on a 'time purchased'
basis by other airlines. The
realism achieved in these
complex and expensive
machines is almost
unbelievable. Reproduced by
courtesy of Rediffusion
Simulation Ltd, is a page from
their brochure. (**222**) shows the
view from the flight deck of a
Boeing 737 simulator
indicating the realism
of it in the
roll mode.
*Rediffusion
Simulation
Ltd*

CGI
visual
system

On board
computer
interface
bays

Motion
system

Visual
system
image
generating
computer

Host computer

Motion system control cabinet

SIGNAL FLOW

222

Novoview
SP CGI visual
system

**TOTAL SOUND
ENVIRONMENT**

MAGGS
onboard
instructor
station

Access drawbridge

Motion system control
cabinet. Incorporates
micro-processor controlled
diagnostics and status
monitoring

Motion system
hydraulic power unit

Hydrostatic six degrees of freedom
system providing realistic motion
cues in response to pilot inputs

COMPUTER ROOM
A High speed 32 bit computer with
associated peripherals and software
B Novoview visual system image
generating computer

223

224
Failure to remove ice from the wings and control surfaces, of a modern airliner can have catastrophic consequences and even prevent take-off. Here, a Trident One is being de-iced at Heathrow Airport.
British Airways

225
A masterpiece of Islamic architecture and at, King Khaled International, Riyadh, Saudi Arabia. Here the air side is seen showing the air bridges.
Saudi Arabia Presidency of Civil Aviation

226
A British Airways TriStar outside the almost completed Terminal 4 at Heathrow.
British Airports Authority

3 Livery

227
The evolution of the American
Airlines logo from the 1930s.
American Airlines

Design consciousness in the aesthetic
sense is a postwar phenomenon. Although
the Bauhaus at Dessau, the famous design
school, whose near neighbours, Junkers,
appeared indifferent to its teaching, was
thriving when civil aviation began in 1919,
little notice was taken of these pioneers of
the modern movement, such as Walter
Gropius and Mies van de Rohe.

The aircraft illustrated in this book will
reveal that livery was not a matter of
concern to the early airlines so long as the
name and registration letters were painted
in large letters on the fuselage, and even
larger letters on the wings. The most
important consideration was the speedy
obliteration of the company name in the
event of an accident!

In Britain, the activities of the Design
and Industries Association, the Society of
Industrial Artists — later to add Designers
to their name — and the Council of
Industrial Design, now the Design Council,
promoted vigorously the graphic art and
product design, interest being stimulated
by the 1946 'Britain Can Make It'
Exhibition and the visually exciting
'Festival of Britain' in 1951.

Frederick Gibberd (later, Sir Frederick)
was responsible for the architectural
design of the new Heathrow terminals and,
gradually, the experts became involved in
the aesthetics of air transport. The names
of James Gardner and Bob Morgan began
to appear in the appropriate journals as
designers of aircraft interiors of high
quality. Among the aircraft styled by them
were the DC-3 'Pionair' class, Vanguard,
Viscount, Airspeed Ambassador
('Elizabethan' class) and the Comet.

Airline standards were rising to levels
which left little competitive edge other
than in passenger appeal through cabin
service and interior design, with the
associated airline publicity and house style
creating external impact. Subtle
considerations such as the reduction in the
'tube look' of a long fuselage were studied
by the designers.

When British Caledonian decided to

extend the lives of their BAC One-Eleven
fleet, the London consultancy Negus and
Negus was called in to up-grade the
aircraft internally. They devised an
ingenious system of lighting which gave
the cabin the appearance of increased
width.

When BEA and BOAC merged in 1974,
Negus and Negus was commissioned to
prepare a scheme for the new British
Airways livery, bearing in mind that there
was healthy rivalry between the staffs of
the two companies. 5,000 employees saw
the proposals and even the most partisan
among them had to admit that the new
livery would be an extension of the style
they knew. The words 'British Airways',
with 14 letters, were too long, in the
opinion of the designers. Contraction to BA
was an acronymous banana skin so, after a
few years, the airline was persuaded to
drop the word 'Airways' leaving a curious
and unhappily truncated effect.

In 1984 British Airways announced its
new corporate identity proposals to be
carried out over two years at a cost of
£42million. The American consultants,
Landor Associates, were commissioned to
carry out the work. As the airline's sales
director put it, 'Our old livery, designed at
the time of the BOAC and BEA merger, was
becoming out-dated and reflected the
brash, bright look of the late 1960s'.

Judgement of such designs must be
subjective, but it is difficult to compare, at
London Airport, the earlier scheme with its
white fuselage top and the Landor scheme,
with its pale grey top, without a strong
feeling that the new one is drab by
comparison with the Negus design.

Strong criticism has been expressed at
the replacement of the well known
Speedbird motif, which first appeared on
the de Havilland Albatross in 1937, with a
coat of arms which, from a distance, is just
a blur on the fin. The BA press hand-out
stated that 'Cities, universities, colleges,
dioceses and abbeys sport their own
distinctive insignia'. One might, perhaps,
be forgiven for wondering what relevance

228
**Qantas advertising
material.** *Qantas*

the fin of an airliner has to those august institutions.

On 25 October 1984 a letter from June Fraser ARCA, President of the Society of Industrial Artists and Designers, and others, appeared in *The Times*:

229

> *Dear Sir*
>
> *It is astounding that with so much design talent available in this country British Airways should reject that resource in favour of an American firm of consultants. It is even more alarming that the corporate identity proposed for our national airline, relying as it does upon a barely distinguishable heraldic device perched incongruously above the remnants of the earlier instantly recognisable and appropriate solution, should shortly, and at great expense to the taxpayer, be the image of this country on the tarmacs of the world.*
>
> *Yours faithfully*
>
> *June Fraser*

As with anything new there are bound to be detractors. Justification for these comments can only be a subjective decision. The new interior designs for the aircraft appear to be much more successful in shades of grey and midnight blue with highlights of red and silver.

There have been some bizarre 'designs' in airline livery. Braniff painted some of the fuselages of its aircraft bright orange, whilst another line adopted psychedelic colours all over. Aloha Airlines, operating in sunny climes as a holiday airline, paints flowers on the rudder — probably a delightful touch in Hawaii but slightly incongruous on a November day at Heathrow!

A regrettable trend is to be observed in the case of some airlines hitherto renowned for their dignified and attractive livery. Pan Am is now sporting its name in very large letters on the fuselage. UAT does the same and, along with, surprisingly, Qantas, now paint the fin and rudder in a strong colour which follows a projected line of the fin leading edge around the side and bottom of the rear fuselage, completely destroying the flowing line of the fuselage. It is to be hoped that these extravagances are temporary aberrations and not trend setters.

From the day when Juan Terry Trippe founded Pan Am in the 1920s and decided that his pilots should abandon their cowboy style garb and follow the sartorial precedent of the merchant navy, staff uniforms have been recognised as an important aspect of airline sales promotion.

Leading fashion designers have been commissioned by airlines and the results have usually been most successful. British Airways has announced new uniforms to complement the new Landor styling of the aircraft. Happily, a British designer, Roland Klein, was used for staff in contact with the customer whilst the André Peters Design House was responsible for other uniforms. Traditionalists will undoubtedly regret the departure of the captain's gold braid in favour of what the line chooses to call 'platinum braid'. Aluminium would have been equally descriptive and the result seems to owe more to the tailoring of company chauffeurs than the timeless traditions of those in command of aeroplanes and the ships which preceded them, and which were adopted so perceptively by Terry Trippe.

There is abundant evidence in travel agents premises and elsewhere that graphic design is taken very seriously and that standards have never been higher, the exception being the airlines of the Soviet block.

Models have been an important element in airline promotion since the 1930s when the famous Northampton model builders, Bassett Lowke Ltd built wooden models of the 'Empire' flying boats and the Armstrong Whitworth Ensign, with, incongruously, a large screw eye in the centre section.

The present ranges of aircraft models are superb examples of craftsmanship in plastics materials.

Unquestionably, good design is good business in the civil aviation industry.

229
The Qantas logo — as seen on a Super Constellation and Boeing 747. *Qantas*

230

232

230
Qantas cabin staff uniforms
from 1948. Left to right:
1948-53; 1953-59; 1959-64;
1964-69; 1969-71; 1971-74;
1974-84. *Qantas*

231
British Airways recent change
of livery didn't just affect the
aircraft as these three
illustrations show. 234 British
Airways Boeing 737-200 in the
new Landor livery. Even in the
original photograph the crest,
which replaces the well known
Speedbird, is a mere smudge
with the motto 'we fly to serve'
quite illegible. It is to be hoped
that, in due course, wiser
counsels will prevail and the
Speedbird reinstated. The line
along the side is red upon a
dark blue surface; with the
diagonal stripe at the front, it is
described as 'the Speedwing'
and is, apparently, a dramatic
and important aspect of the
design.

232
Shows the Super Club interior,
a more pleasing effect.

233
Various examples of
typography. *British Airways*

234 , 235
Probably no other industry
promotes the concept of
'corporate identity' so
purposefully and effectively as
the airlines. Among the leaders
is SAS. The brochure which
illustrates all aspects of their
latest designs contains an
interesting insight into the
philosophy of the airline and
their reasons for spending
$15million. Part of the answer

to the question 'Why?' is, 'It is
probably one of the wisest
investments we have made
since we set out to become ''The
Business Man's Airline'', the
preferred airline of the frequent
business traveller. . . It is also a
necessary move in extending
the competitive life span of our
aircraft, primarily our DC-9s,
so that we can continue flying
them throughout the 1980s,
with added customer appeal.
  'Today, other airlines are
investing several hundred
million kronor to replace a
single DC-9. We are
rejuvenating all 60 of ours, plus
all the other aircraft in our fleet,
for just a fraction of the price of
one new airliner. . . The
uniforms were designed by
Calvin Klein, known for a
universal style which is not
limited to only one country or
culture. We placed special
emphasis on the uniforms not
only because they are part of
our image, but also because
they must be the working
clothes of thousands of people
for years to come. They also
reflect both our dedication to
service and our personnel's
pride in their profession.'
SAS uniforms illustrated are:
(**235**) Cabin attendant indoor
uniform 1971 and (**234**)
winter uniform 1983.
  The re-styled cabin interiors
are particularly elegant. The
Euroclass cabin has seats of a
sculptured quality with two-
tone dark blue upholstery
relieved by fine horizontal
bands in peacock green and
light blue. The carpet is dark
blue with a fine green and red
fleck in it. *SAS*

234

236, 237, 238, 239
Swissair has always, predictably, presented a stylish image. (**236**) The famous Nellie Diener in her 1934 uniform with peaked cap at a rakish angle, in front of a Curtiss Condor.

(**237**) A flight attendant, sadly anonymous, in the uniform worn from 1946 to 1948, with a Douglas DC-3 Dakota.

(**238** and **239**) Three more ladies, even more sadly, anonymous, wearing indoor and outdoor uniform of 1970 vintage. *Swissair*

240

241

240, 241, 242, 243
Alitalia, with its Italian haute
couture association has always
taken the design of staff
uniforms seriously. Illustrated
are (**240-243**) those of 1960,
1966, 1969/71 and 1977/79
respectively. Some of the
photographs also show the
airline's predilection for
parallel lines as a styling
feature, to the extent of creating
the letters of its name in this
way.
Alitalia

242

244, 245
BOAC uniforms: (**244**) an exotic sari worn by an attendant on a Boeing 707 on the Indian routes. (**245**) BOAC's Cabin Service Officer/training demonstrating a range of products used on the Atlantic routes in 1971.
British Airways

246
Compare the new livery with that of the BEA design of the 1950s where the letters BEA were used in a red square which looked totally incongruous in relation to the sleek lines of the aircraft. *British Airways*

247, 248
247 and **248** show American Airlines styles of 1933 and 1984.

249, 250
Certain company emblems, or logotypes, as they have become known, have, through sheer merit, been perpetuated over the years. The Lufthansa 'flying crane' is the oldest, shown in the photograph on the rudder of a 1919 AEG-J11 of Deutsche Luft Reederei and on the fin of a modern DC-10. It will also be noticed upon the captain's cap badge. Short back and sides haircuts do not seem to be mandatory in Lufthansa!

250

251
KLM and Monarch use stylised forms of a crown, the KLM version, probably derives from the unprecedented gesture by Queen Wilhelmina when she graciously permitted the new airline to commence operations in 1919, with the prefix 'Royal' in its title. Monarch use a form ingeniously embodying the initial 'M', shown in the fin of their Boeing 757. *Monarch*

251

4 World Development of Civil Aviation

All Scheduled Services of International and Domestic Airlines

Year	Kilometres flown* (millions)	% increase	Passengers carried† (millions)	% increase	Passengers kilometres† (millions)	% increase	Freight tonne/km† (millions)	% increase	Average passengers per aircraft (number)*
1937	265		2.5		1,410		na		5
1947	1,140	330	21.0	740	19,000	1,247	270	—	17
1950	1,440	26	31.0	48	28,000	47	730	270	19
1960	3,110	116	106.0	242	109,000	289	2,170	197	35
1970	7,005	125	312.0	194	460,000	322	11,950	451	55
1980	9,310	33	748.0	140	1,089,000	137	29,130	144	100
1984	9,820	5.5	832.0	11.2	1,265,000	16.2	38,910	33.6	110

* Excludes USSR.
†Includes USSR from 1970.
Statistics by courtesy of the International Civil Aviation Organisation.

5 Airliner Development, 1919~82

Proto-type first flight	Aircraft	All-up weight (lb)	No of engs	Total hp or thrust in lb	Pass-engers	Cruising speed (mph)	Range miles	Wing area (sq ft)	Wing loading (lb/sq ft)
1919	Junkers F13	3,814	1	185	4	110	404	473.6	8.1
1919	Handley Page W8B	12,000	2	700	14	100	500	145.6	8.2
1919	Vickers Vimy Comm'l	12,500	2	720	10	94	450	1,330	9.4
1925	Fokker FVIII 3M	11,684	3	900	10	110	746	729	16.0
1926	A. W. Argosy	19,200	3	1,230	28	95	520	1,873	10.3
1929	Junkers G38	52,910	4	3,000	34	129	1,181	3,229	16.4
1930	Handley Page 42	28,000	4	1,960	24	95	500	2,990	9.4
1932	A. W. Atalanta	21,000	4	1,500	11	118	640	1,285	16.3
1933	Boeing 247	12,650	2	1,100	10	155	485	863	14.66
1934	Douglas DC-2	18,560	2	1,440	14	198	1,000	939	19.8
1937	Focke Wulf 200	37,478	4	3,320	26	228	932	1,292	29.0
1937	D. H. Albatross	29,500	4	2,100	21	210	1,040	1,078	27.4
1941	Avro Lancastrian	65,000	4	6,560	9	210	1,660	1,297	50.2
1947	Airspeed Ambassador	52,500	2	5,250	60	272	1,550	1,200	43.9
1949	D. H. Comet 1A	115,000	4	20,000	44	490	2,000	2,015	57.1
1950	Lockheed Super Constellation	137,000	4	13,000 (hp)	99	355	4,620	1,650	83.3
1950	Vickers Viscount 700	50,000	4	6,160 (ehp*)	40	316	950	963	51.9
1951	Douglas DC 6B	107,000	4	9,600	102	315	3,005	1,463	73.1
1952	Bristol Britannia 102	155,000	4	15,480	139	335	3,800	2,075	74.7
1954	Boeing 707-320c	336,000	4	72,000	219	600	4,000	2,892	116.2
1962	D. H. Trident III	115,000	3	29,550	103	589	1,094	1,358	84.7
1962	Vickers VC 10 Super	335,000	4	90,000	151	581	4,720	2,932	114.3
1963	Boeing 727-200	173,000 to 208,000	3	48,000	189	600	2,800	1,650	104.8
1969	Boeing 747-300	775,000 to 833,000	4	187,800	496	583	5,500	5,500	140.9
1969	Concorde	408,000	4	152,200 (+17%†)	100	1,354	4,090	3,856	105.8
1970	Lockheed Tri-Star	430,000	3	126,000	400	599	3,305	3,456	124.4
1972	Airbus 300-600	365,750	2	112,000	375	550	4,900	2,799	130.7
1982	Boeing 767-200	300,000 to 345,000	2	96,000	290	528	3,200 to 5,600	3,050	113.1

* ehp — Equivalent shaft hp.
† +17% when re-heat is operating.
The date given is that of the first flight of the prototype, not that of the sub-type quoted.
Note: Performance figures are usually qualified by other factors, which for brevity have been left out. Data given may therefore vary from other published data based upon different factors.

6 Cruising Speeds, 1919~80

1 **Junkers F13**
2 **Fokker FVII/3M**
3 **Junkers G38**
4 **Handley Page 42**
5 **Boeing 247**
6 **Douglas DC-2**
7 **Focke Wulf 200**
8 **De Havilland Albatross**
9 **Airspeed Ambassador**
10 **De Havilland Comet**
11 **Vickers Viscount-700**
12 **Boeing 707-320c**
13 **Vickers VC 10**
14 **Boeing 747-300**
15 **Concorde**

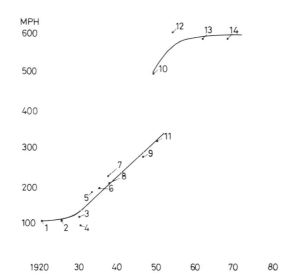

(15) 1354 mph.

7 Operating Ranges, 1919~80

1 **Junkers F13**
2 **Fokker FVII/3M**
3 **Junkers G38**
4 **Handley Page 42**
5 **Boeing 247**
6 **Douglas DC-2**
7 **Focke Wulf 200**
8 **De Havilland Albatross**
9 **Airspeed Ambassador**
10 **De Havilland Comet**
11 **Vickers Viscount-700**
12 **Boeing 707-320c**
13 **Vickers VC 10**
14 **Boeing 747-300**
15 **Concorde**

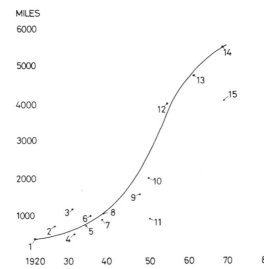

8 Passenger Capacity, 1919~80

1   Junkers F13
2   Fokker FVII/3M
3   Junkers G38
4   Handley Page 42
5   Boeing 247
6   Douglas DC-2
7   Focke Wulf 200
8   De Havilland Albatross
9   Airspeed Ambassador
10 De Havilland Comet
11 Vickers Viscount-700
12 Boeing 707-320c
13 Vickers VC 10
14 Boeing 747-300
15 Concorde

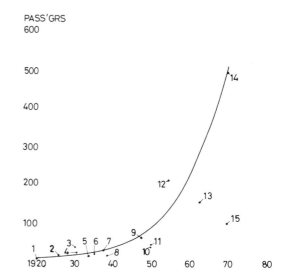

9 Wing Loading, 1919~80

1   Junkers F13
2   Fokker FVII/3M
3   Junkers G38
4   Handley Page 42
5   Boeing 247
6   Douglas DC-2
7   Focke Wulf 200
8   De Havilland Albatross
9   Airspeed Ambassador
10 De Havilland Comet
11 Vickers Viscount-700
12 Boeing 707-320c
13 Vickers VC 10
14 Boeing 747-300
15 Concorde

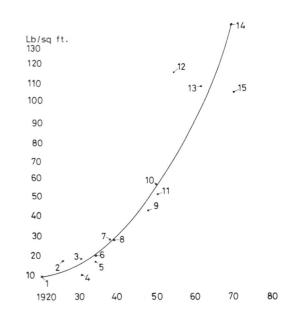